TYRANNOSAURUS LEX

TYRANNOSAURUS LEX

THE MARVELOUS
BOOK OF
PALINDROMES,
ANAGRAMS,
AND OTHER
DELIGHTFUL AND
OUTRAGEOUS
WORDPLAY

Rod L. Evans, Ph.D.

A PERIGEE BOOK

A PERIGEE BOOK
Published by the Penguin Group
Penguin Group (USA) Inc.
375 Hudson Street, New York, New York 10014, USA

Penguin Group (Canada), 90 Eglinton Avenue East, Suite 700, Toronto, Ontario M4P 2Y3, Canada
(a division of Pearson Penguin Canada Inc.) • Penguin Books Ltd., 80 Strand, London WC2R 0RL,
England • Penguin Group Ireland, 25 St. Stephen's Green, Dublin 2, Ireland (a division of Penguin
Books Ltd.) • Penguin Group (Australia), 250 Camberwell Road, Camberwell, Victoria 3124, Australia
(a division of Pearson Australia Group Pty. Ltd.) • Penguin Books India Pvt. Ltd., 11 Community
Centre, Panchsheel Park, New Delhi—110 017, India • Penguin Group (NZ), 67 Apollo Drive,
Rosedale, Auckland 0632, New Zealand (a division of Pearson New Zealand Ltd.) • Penguin Books
(South Africa) (Pty.) Ltd., 24 Sturdee Avenue, Rosebank, Johannesburg 2196, South Africa

Penguin Books Ltd., Registered Offices: 80 Strand, London WC2R 0RL, England

While the author has made every effort to provide accurate telephone numbers and Internet addresses
at the time of publication, neither the publisher nor the author assumes any responsibility for errors
or for changes that occur after publication. Further, the publisher does not have any control over and
does not assume any responsibility for author or third-party websites or their content.

First edition: June 2012

Library of Congress Cataloging-in-Publication Data

Evans, Rod L., 1956–
Tyrannosaurus lex : the marvelous book of palindromes, anagrams, and
other delightful and outrageous wordplay / Rod L. Evans.—1st ed.
        p.   cm.
"A Perigee book."
Includes bibliographical references.
ISBN 978-0-399-53749-3
1. Palindromes.   2. Plays on words.   3. Anagrams.   4. Word games.   I. Title.
PN6371.E93 2012
793.734—dc23
2012002319

PRINTED IN THE UNITED STATES OF AMERICA

10   9   8   7   6   5   4   3   2   1

Most Perigee books are available at special quantity discounts for bulk purchases for
sales promotions, premiums, fund-raising, or educational use. Special books, or book
excerpts, can also be created to fit specific needs. For details, write: Special Markets,
Penguin Group (USA) Inc., 375 Hudson Street, New York, New York 10014.

ACKNOWLEDGMENTS

My deep thanks go to my literary agents, Sheree Bykofsky and Janet Rosen; my excellent editor at Perigee, Meg Leder, who has always believed in me and given me invaluable guidance; the talented freelance copyeditor Candace Levy; my friend Justin Gruver, who typed much of the manuscript; my friend Robin Hudgins, who also typed a good portion of the manuscript and formatted it; my friend Rob Stewart and colleague Elaine Dawson, who also copyedited the manuscript; investment adviser and prolific author John Train, whose classic *John Train's Most Remarkable Names* not only inspired my interest in people's names but also served as the principal source for my subsection "Names That Belong or Have Belonged to Real People"; and last but not least, Richard Lederer, whose work has inspired me. This book has been enriched by the hard work of many people. I am grateful.

CONTENTS

INTERLUDE 2
AN ATHLETIC BREAK: WORDPLAY INVOLVING
SPORTS FIGURES' MALAPROPISMS AND
UNUSUAL NAMES IN SPORTS

INTERLUDE 3
A MUSICAL BREAK: WORDPLAY INVOLVING
MISHEARD LYRICS, PUNS, AND
PALINDROMES IN MUSIC

INTERLUDE 4
A NOMINAL BREAK:
WORDPLAY INVOLVING THE
OUTRAGEOUS NAMES OF REAL PEOPLE

INTERLUDE 5
A COMMERCIAL BREAK: WORDPLAY INVOLVING PUNS AND FUNNY HOMOPHONES USED IN BUSINESSES

INTERLUDE 6
A LITERARY BREAK: WORDPLAY INVOLVING AUTHORS' NAMES AND BOOK TITLES

INTRODUCTION

Webster's Collegiate Dictionary defines *wordplay* as "verbal wit." Wordplay involves manipulating or calling attention to letters, sounds, or meanings. When most people think of wordplay, they think of anagrams and palindromes, which are indeed excellent examples. Take *Albert Einstein.* Rearrange the letters, and you can get the anagram *ten elite brains.* Rearrange *dormitory,* and you can get *dirty room.* Now consider the palindrome. The sentence *Dennis and Edna sinned* spells the same forward and backward (after suitably spacing some letters). *Do geese see God?* and *lonely Tylenol* are similarly versatile.

Although anagrams and palindromes are important and delightful examples of verbal wit, they represent only two large rooms of a mansion in which one will find not only wordplay but also scholars, authors, and especially comedians. In fact, some of the finest wordplay comes from comedians. The comedian Steven Wright once said, "There will be a rain dance on Friday, weather permitting." The more one reflects on the line, the wittier it becomes. The rain dance, a serious religious ritual used in urgent situations, is treated in the funny line as a nonurgent social event, such as a cotillion. The qualification *weather permitting* makes the joke, humorously contradicting what precedes it. Obviously, the purpose of a rain dance is to produce rain. If it rains, there is no need to have the dance. Yet the qualification *weather permitting* treats the rain dance as if it were a social engagement whose purpose has nothing to do with the weather.

Steven Wright's joke about a rain dance illustrates that language is deeply connected to culture and that a simple-looking one-liner can require a good deal of linguistic and cultural knowledge to appreciate. To understand the joke, the listener must know, among other things, that a rain dance is radically different from a recreational dance. Similarly, if someone says that he was so poor that he couldn't afford even a birthday suit, his joke requires understanding that a birthday suit (nakedness) is radically different from a suit of clothes. Indeed, a birthday suit is no more a suit than a decoy duck is a duck. The word *birthday* in *birthday suit*, the word *decoy* in *decoy duck*, and the word *counterfeit* in *counterfeit money* negate the nouns they modify. Each is an example of an alienans, to which a chapter of this book is devoted.

Verbal wit often involves irony, creating an expectation only to dash it, as when comedian George Carlin once said, "In America, anyone can become president. That's the problem." The statement that in America anyone can become president is taken from its customary context, in which it is used to support the claim that political power in America has become democratized to the point at which one can become president without being born to privilege. Carlin's "That's the problem" implies that democratization, far from being an unqualified good, can lead to mediocrity or even incompetence.

Wordplay is a natural part of language and is associated with riddles, puzzles, games, puns, jokes, double entendres, and even linguistic confusion (as in mala-propisms). It involves viewing or treating language as an art form, as a source of entertainment. We can find it almost everywhere, including homes, schools, of-fices, businesses, and even public restrooms (graffiti). The advertisement and bumper sticker "I ♥ NY" is based on a rebus, a message involving words and pic-tures. A radiator repair business whose slogan is "Best place in town to take a leak" is also using wordplay—the pun.

Indeed, the pun, like some other forms of wordplay, has existed since ancient times. Puns, for example, are often found in Sanskrit and sometimes in Latin (as in the plays of the Roman playwright Plautus, known for making up and changing the meanings of words to cre-ate puns). What's more, palindromes also existed in ancient times, as evidenced by the following graffito, found in the remains of the ancient Roman town of Herculaneum, buried by volcanic ash: "*Sator Arepo tenet opera rotas*," which can be translated as "The sower Arepo works with the help of a wheel." Further, anagrams were used by the Greek poet Lycophron in about 260 B.C.E. Anagrams, then, are an ancient art, as logologists remind us by telling us that the word *ana-grams* can be transposed into *ars magna* (Latin for "great art").

Although wordplay was practiced in ancient times, it has become increasingly scientific, especially since the 1960s. A man who deserves credit for helping to put wordplay on a scientific footing is Dmitri Borgmann, who, in 1965, published *Language on Vacation: An Olio of Orthographical Oddities*. An excellent work on pal-indromes, anagrams, and many other forms of visual wordplay involving recognizing and manipulating patterns of letters, it presented wordplay in a scientific light, as a discipline with its own logic, concepts, and vocabulary. Borgmann's groundbreaking book earned him the title "Father of Logology," popularizing a term for recreational linguistics.

In 1968, Borgmann founded *Word Ways: The Journal of Recreational Linguistics*, the first magazine devoted to all forms of wordplay. In 1969, Howard Bergerson came to edit *Word Ways* and later wrote an influential book on palindromes and anagrams, appropriately titled *Palindromes and Anagrams*. From 1970 to 2006 Ross Eckler took over the editorship and publication of *Word Ways*, which has been enormously important to wordplay and which is still published quarterly. To get an idea of the hundreds of forms of wordplay, you can pick up Dave Morice's *The Dictionary of Wordplay*.

Although *Word Ways* has always been important to scholars and serious students of recreational linguistics (logology), the most widely read material on wordplay since the 1980s is probably from Richard Lederer, whose 1987 book *Anguished English*, featuring real-life linguistic bloopers, was read by Jay Leno on *The Tonight Show* for eight minutes. The book became a huge bestseller and helped launch Dell's series Intrepid Linguistic Library, tapping into, and helping to build, a popular market for logology. His subsequent books, such as *Get Thee to a Punnery, Crazy English*, and *The Word Circus* have brought logology to a large readership. Lederer skillfully does what logologists aspire to do: He presents wordplay in such a way as to combine scholarship, popular culture, and humor. I hope to follow in his footsteps.

A NOTE ABOUT CONTENT AND ORGANIZATION

This book consists of chapters, interludes, sidebars, and an appendix. Each chapter centers on some form of wordplay, such as anagrams, palindromes, or puns. Following the last chapter is an appendix of more than 400 funny, outlandish, or outrageous names listed in real phone and address directories and aggregated in Zaba Search (zabasearch.com). Most of the names are entertaining homophones (intentional or accidental) of other words. You'll find, for example, *Curtis E. Counts* (courtesy counts), *Anita Break* (I need a break), *Laura Lynn Hardy* (Laurel and Hardy) and hundreds of others; some of these homophones are rude or risqué.

Each chapter is a room in the mansion of wordplay. Although the book represents a broad cross-section of the subject, it is far from an exhaustive treatment. You already know about its having puns, anagrams, and palindromes. What's more, you've been exposed to some material I consider sentences with ambushes, paraprosdokians, as in comedian Stephen Colbert's line, "If I am reading this graph correctly—I'd be very surprised."

Another room in the mansion of wordplay is that of acronyms, pronounceable abbreviations, such as *NATO*. This book unveils some surprising acronyms, such as *TURD*, which can stand for **t**imed **u**niversal **r**earward **d**estroyer, an airburst bomb whose acronym gives new meaning to the expression *drop a TURD*.

Another room is that of malapropisms, words misused for similar-sounding ones, often producing humorous or ridiculous results, as when TV's Archie Bunker called a minstrel show a "menstrual show." Near the room of malapropisms is the room of eggcorns, idiosyncratic but semantically motivated substitutions of words or phrases that sound similar or identical in the speaker's dialect. The substitutions differ from the customary expressions but make sense and can be even creative in the context. The phenomenon got its name because a woman said *eggcorn* or *egg corn* for *acorn*. The relevant connection (albeit tenuous) between eggs and acorns is their shapes. There are better examples of eggcorns than the primordial eggcorn (namely, *eggcorn*), as when people erroneously but creatively call Alzheimer's disease "old-timer's disease," sickle cell anemia "sick-as-hell anemia," or maiden name "mating name."

Another room in the mansion, next to that of eggcorns, is the room of oronyms. An oronym is a pair of phrases that sound the same or similar but differ in meaning and spelling, as in *stuffy nose* and *stuff he knows* and in *some others* and *some mothers*.

Next to the room of oronyms is that of mondegreens, aural malapropisms, which are mishearings or misinterpretations of phrases that sound like the correct phrases. Although mondegreens can stem from misheard poetry and other speech (such as the Pledge of Allegiance), they are common in music. By the way, a mondegreen in music that has confused literally millions of people stems from a famous cover of a Bruce Springsteen song by the Manfred Mann's Earth Band "Blinded by the Light." Almost everybody thinks that the words "revved up like a deuce [coupe]" are "wrapped up like a douche."

Still another room, among the dozens in the mansion, is that of portmanteau words, blends of two or more words, such as *smog* (*smoke* and *fog*). In this book you'll find recent portmanteaux, such as *sexiled* (for *sex* and *exile*), describing the condition of being unable to go into one's room, dorm, or apartment because one's roommate needs privacy for sex, and *southmaw* (from *southpaw* and *maw*), describing one who eats primarily with the left side of one's mouth.

The wordplay in this book is not only multifarious but also multilayered. For example, in the interlude on literary wordplay, I comment on book titles, creating additional wordplay in the form of puns or double entendres. What's more, in the appendix, when I note where the persons listed reside or have resided, there is sometimes a happy coincidence between the name and the location, as in Jordan Rivers, who has resided in Eau Claire (clear water), Wisconsin.

If this book entertains you and gives you a bit more insight into the vast panorama of language variously known as logology, recreational linguistics, or wordplay, I shall be happy.

Rod L. Evans

TYRANNOSAURUS LEX

CHAPTER 1

Aptly Scrambled Words: Aptanagramy

Words generally don't have many places in which to hide. When you say a word, it is out. Words do, however, have one especially good hiding place: inside other words—the last place most people would think to find them. How many "career politicians" would look for "nice parasitic role" to describe themselves?

Whole words can be hidden in other words by rearranging their letters, as when *news* becomes *sewn*. Such transformations are called anagrams, and *aptanagram* (ap-TAN-uh-gram) can be used to describe an anagram of an extraordinary kind. As its name suggests, it's an anagram that forms an apt word (phrase or sentence).

Although most of the following anagrams are apt, some of them aren't indisputable aptanagrams but are highly partisan.

a decimal point = I'm a dot in place
a diet = I'd eat
a sentence of death = faces one at the end
a shoplifter = has to pilfer
a stitch in time saves nine = is this meant as incentive?
a telephone girl = repeating hello

an ordained minister = I ranted, "Admire no sin!"

angered = enraged

antidemocratic = dictator came in

asteroid threats = disaster to Earth

astronomers = moon starers

belligerents = rebelling set

breasts = bra sets

Britney Spears = best PR in years

caste = a sect

certainly not = can't rely on it

Christmas = trims cash

Clint Eastwood = old west action

clothespins = so let's pinch

coins kept = in pockets

compassionateness = stamps one as so nice

confessional = on scale of sin

considerate = care is noted

contemplation = on mental topic

contradiction = accord not in it

conversation = voices rant on

David Letterman = nerd amid late TV *or* terminal
    dead TV

debit card = bad credit

dormitory = dirty room

election results = lie, let's recount

eleven + two = twelve + one

endearment = tender name

Episcopalianism = claim a pope is sin

fir cones = conifers

George W. Bush = he grew bogus

God save us all = salvaged soul

Guinness draught = naughtiness drug

hibernates = the bear's in

hot water = worth tea

Howard Stern = wonder trash
I think; therefore, I am = I fear to think I'm here
indomitableness = endless ambition
iPod lover = poor devil
large breasts = great braless
laxative = exit lava
listen = silent
Madonna Louise Ciccone = one cool dance musician *or* occasional nude income
Margaret Thatcher = that great charmer
mother-in-law = woman Hitler
my ideal time = immediately
Nancy Pelosi = n-sane policy
negation = get a no in
no admittance = contaminated
ocean = canoe
older and wiser = I learned words
one's birthday suit = this nudity so bare
orators hate = a sore throat
Osama bin Laden = a bad man (no lies)
parishioners = I hire parsons
postmaster = stamp store
Presbyterian = best in prayer
President Bush of the USA = a fresh one, but he's stupid
President Clinton of the USA = to copulate, he finds interns
Princess Diana = end is a car spin *or* ascend in Paris
protectionism = cite no imports
punishment = nine thumps
rats and mice = in cat's dream
Richard Milhous Nixon = his climax ruined honor
Ronald Reagan = an oral danger
Ronald Wilson Reagan = insane Anglo warlord
Saddam Hussein = UN's said he's mad

schoolmaster = the classroom

school student = tends to slouch

semaphore = see arm hop

Sharon Stone = ass on throne

slot machines = cash lost in 'em

Spiro Agnew (*President Nixon's disgraced vice president*) = grow a penis *or* grow a spine

sycophant = acts phony

tantrums = must rant

television ads = enslave idiots

Ten Commandments = can't mend most men

the centenarians = I can hear ten tens

the compulsory education law = you must learn; police do watch

the Declaration of Independence = a co-penned edict held nation free

the eyes = they see

the lost paradise = earth's ideal spot

the maternity hospital = type that mothers ail in

the nudist colony = no untidy clothes

the U.S. Library of Congress = it's only for research bugs

Tom Cruise = I'm so cuter

Western Union = no wire unsent

CHAPTER 2

Santa Vs. Satan: Antigrams

When the letters of words or phrases are rearranged to form words or phrases opposite in meaning (antonyms), antigrams result. Because it is easier to find words related in meaning to other words than words that carry contrary or opposite meanings, antigrams are rarer than apt anagrams. One of the most famous antigrams is *Santa/Satan*. Some of the following examples have contrasting rather than opposite meanings.

antagonist ≠ not against
a sun worshiper ≠ I shun Ra's power
butchers ≠ cut herbs
customers ≠ store scum
demoniacal ≠ a docile man
diplomacy ≠ mad policy
dormitories ≠ tidier rooms
dynamited ≠ a tidy mend
earliest ≠ rise late
evangelists ≠ evil's agents
filled ≠ ill-fed
forty-five ≠ over fifty
funeral ≠ real fun
gratitude ≠ I get a turd
honestly ≠ on the sly

honorees ≠ no heroes
infernos ≠ nonfires
inroads ≠ no raids
lemonade ≠ demon ale
maidenly ≠ men daily
marital ≠ martial
mentors ≠ monster
militarism ≠ I limit arms
misfortune ≠ it's more fun
nominate ≠ I name not
persecuted ≠ due respect
protectionism ≠ nice to imports
reforestation ≠ no fair to trees
restful ≠ fluster
saintliness ≠ entails sins
Santa ≠ Satan
spittoon ≠ it's no pot
sweltering heat ≠ the winter gales
teacher ≠ cheater
the morning after ≠ in great form then
the parsonage ≠ so pagan there
unite ≠ untie
united ≠ untied
violence ≠ nice love
within earshot ≠ I won't hear this

CHAPTER 3

A Group Called CREEP Helped Reelect President Nixon: Acronyms

An acronym is a word formed from the letters or syllables or arbitrary parts of expressions or phrases. In short, acronyms are pronounceable abbreviations constituting words. Acronyms can be distinguished from initialisms, in which a group of letters used as an abbreviation for a name or an expression is pronounced by naming each letter, as in *BBC* (British Broadcasting Corporation) or *PBS* (Public Broadcasting System). Acronyms, as said, form new words and are pronounced as words. Accordingly, we pronounce *NATO* NAY-toh and don't pronounce the abbreviation as en-ay-tee-oh. We do, however, pronounce *UK* by naming each letter: you-kay. That expression, then, is an initialism.

Although initialisms and to some extent acronyms have existed for centuries, they've received little systematic analysis until recent times.

The Hebrew language has a long history of acronyms. Indeed, the Hebrew Bible (what Christians call the Old Testament) is known as TANAKH, an acronym composed from the initial letters of the Hebrew names of the three major sections: Torah (the Pentateuch, or Five Books of Moses), Nevi'im (the prophets), and Kethuvim (the writings).

Further, many medieval and post-medieval rabbinical figures are designated by their acronyms, such as Rambama (aka Maimonides, from the initial letters of his full name Rabbi Moshe ben Maimon) and Rashi (Rabbi Schlomo Yitzchaki). (For a good scholarly book on acronyms, see Don Hauptman's *Acronymania*.)

One can find initialisms for American companies in the nineteenth century, as when the Richmond, Fredericksburg & Potomac (a railroad connecting Richmond, Virginia, to Washington, DC) was called RF&P. Acronyms, unlike initialisms, were almost unheard of in American businesses until the twentieth century, as when *Nabisco* was first used to describe the National Biscuit Company, or when, much later, *Sunoco* came to describe the Sun Company, Inc., from the earlier name Sun Oil Company.

ACRONYMS USED IN NAMES OF COMMERCIAL PRODUCTS

Atra = **a**utomatic **t**racking **r**azor **a**ction

canola oil = **Can**ada **o**il **l**ow **ac**id

Corvair = **Corv**ette + Bel **Air**

Fiat = **F**abrica **I**taliana **A**utomobili, **T**orini

Maalox = **ma**gnesium **al**uminum hydr**ox**ide

Qantas = **Q**ueensland **a**nd **N**orthern **T**erritories **A**erial **S**ervices

Sanka = **san**s (*French for "without"*) + **ca**ffeine (*I know; it should probably be Sanca.*)

Sentra = **sen**try + cen**tra**l

Swatch = **Sw**iss + **watch**
Toshiba = **To**kyo + **Shiba**ura (*electrical company*)

FUNNY, CLEVER, AND RUDE ACRONYMS

ACNE = **A**ction **C**ommittee for **N**arcotics **E**ducation; **A**laskans **C**oncerned for **N**eglected **E**nvironments

ANUS = **A**merican **N**ihilist **U**nderground **S**ociety

BITCH = **b**abe **i**n **t**otal **c**ontrol of **h**erself; **b**eautiful **i**ntelligent **t**alented **c**reative **h**onest; **B**lack **I**ntelligence **T**est of **C**ultural **H**omogeneity

BURP = **b**achelor of **u**rban and **r**egional **p**lanning; **b**ig **u**gly **r**ock **p**iece (*LEGO slang*); **B**randeis **U**niversity **R**ecycling **P**rogram

COYOTE = **C**all **O**ff **Y**our **O**ld **T**ired **E**thics (*a group calling for decriminalizing prostitution, pimping, and pandering and destigmatizing sex workers, including strippers, phone sex operators, and adult film performers*)

CRAP = **c**heap **r**edundant **a**ssorted **p**roducts; **C**itizens **R**aging **a**gainst **P**hones (*Grand Theft Auto*)

CRASH = **C**anadians for **R**esponsible **a**nd **S**afe **H**ighways; **C**ommunity **R**esources **a**gainst **S**treet **H**oodlums (*Los Angeles Police Department*)

CREEP = **C**ommittee for the **Re**-**E**lection of the **P**resident (*President Nixon's 1972 campaign organization*)

CRUD = **C**oloradans **R**unning **U**ltra **D**istances

DASTARD = **d**estroyer **a**nti-**s**ubmarine **t**ransportation **ar**ray **d**etection

FART = **F**air & **A**ccurate **R**eporting on **T**elevision; **F**armers **a**gainst **R**idiculous **T**axes (New Zealand); **f**ast **a**ction **r**esponse **t**eam; **F**athers **a**gainst **R**ude

Television (*Futurama cartoons*); Federal Acronym Registration Team (*The Daily Show*); fire alarm response team; fire and rescue team; fireman's annual river trip; Flatulent Airborne Reaction Team (*George Carlin*)

FOOL = foundations of object-oriented languages; free object-oriented license

GERM = geochemical earth reference model; global equity risk management

GOO = gastric outlet obstruction; Grand Ole Opry (*Nashville, Tennessee*); Gulf of Oman

HALT = Help Abolish Legal Tyranny; Horse Assisted Learning and Therapy (*Summerfield, Florida*)

ITCH = Information Technology Can Help (*United Kingdom*); Institute for Total Carpet Hygiene (*Henley-In-Arden, United Kingdom*)

LISP = Linked Investment Service Provider (*financial administration*); location identifier separation protocol (*computer networking*)

MUFF = Melbourne Underground Film Festival (*Australia*); Men United for Fantasy Football; Montreal Underground Film Festival

NERD = network event recording device; non-erosive reflux disease

PENIS = proton-enhanced nuclear induction spectroscopy

PIMP = paper in my pocket; party in my pants; pee(ing) in my pants; personal Internet mail processor; pipeline integrity management plan (*petrochemical industry*); player in management position; positive intake manifold pressure

PITS = Payload Integration Test Set (*NASA*)

PUS = Performance under Stress (*San Francisco Theater Group*); public understanding of science

ACRONYMS THAT HAVE BECOME UNCAPITALIZED

dopa = **d**ihydr**o**xy**p**henyl**a**line

fido = **f**reaks **i**rregulars **d**efects **o**ddities

gox = **g**aseous **ox**ygen (*similar to lox = liquid oxygen*)

laser = **l**ight **a**mplification by **s**timulated **e**mission of radiation

maser = **m**icrowave **a**mplification by **s**timulated **e**mission of radiation

parsec = **par**allax **sec**ond

radar = **ra**dio **d**etection **a**nd **r**anging

scuba = **s**elf-**c**ontained **u**nderwater **b**reathing **ap**paratus

zip = **Z**one **I**mprovement **P**lan

SATAN = **s**atellite **a**utomatic **t**racking **an**tenna; **s**ecurity **a**dministrator **t**ool for **a**nalyzing **n**etworks

SCRAM = **s**upersonic **c**ombustion **ram**jet (*a type of jet engine*)

SCUM = **S**aboteurs and **C**riminals **U**nited in **M**ayhem (*James Bond Jr. cartoons*); **s**elf-**c**entered **u**rban **m**ale; **S**outh **C**oast **U**nited **M**otorcyclists

SLOB = *Secret Language of Birds* (*Ian Anderson CD*); **s**ecured **l**ease **o**bligation **b**ond; **s**eparate **l**ine **o**f **b**usiness (*rules for testing retirement plans*); **s**low **b**all (*cricket ball pitch*)

SMIRK = **S**ix **M**eter **I**nternational **R**adio **K**lub

SMITE = **S**uspected **M**alicious **I**nsider **T**hreat **E**limination (*U.S. Department of Defense*)

SNOT = **s**tuds **n**ot **o**n **t**op (*LEGO building method*)

SPERM = **s**ocial **p**olitical **e**conomic **r**eligious **m**ilitary (*method of categorizing historical events and ideas*)

SPIT = **s**igned **p**erformances **i**n **t**heater; **S**outh **P**adre Island, Texas; **S**pace **P**lanning and Implementation Team; **S**upporters of **P**olitically **I**ncorrect **T**opics

STOP = **S**trategy **T**argeting **O**rganized **P**iracy

SUX = **Si**o**ux** City (*Iowa; airport code*)

TURD = **t**imed **u**niversal **r**earward **d**estroyer (*an airburst bomb*)

WIMP = **w**eakly **i**nteracting **m**assive **p**articles

ZIT = **Z**one **I**nformation **T**able

CHAPTER 4

The Truth Behind SOS, Posh, and the Amber Alert: Bacronyms

A bacronym (*backward* and *acronym*) is a phrase or sentence constructed from the letters of a word that is treated as an acronym but wasn't originally an acronym, as when the word *Ford* (the car brand) was humorously represented as standing for "**f**ix **o**r **r**epair **d**aily." Indeed, many acronyms are humorous, especially those that pejoratively describe products, as when people say that *DVD* stands for "**d**elivers **v**irtual **d**reck," and when they used to say that *VHS* stood for "**v**irtually **h**opeless **s**ignal" rather than for "**v**ertical **he**lical **s**can."

Although many bacronyms are humorous, many are serious, including some based on folk etymologies, popular but erroneous explanations of the origins of words. *Posh* is often incorrectly believed to stand for "**p**ort **o**ut, **s**tarboard **h**ome," supposedly describing the cooler, north-facing cabins taken by aristocratic or important passengers traveling with the Peninsular and Oriental Steam Navigation Company from Britain to India and back. Although there are different theories about the origin of the word *posh*, it wasn't created as an acronym.

Another popular bacronym that stems from a misunderstanding is expressed by the claim that *SOS* stands for "**S**ave **o**ur **s**hip." In reality, it doesn't stand for any words but was chosen because it is simple to express in Morse code (three dots, three dashes, three dots).

Finally, many people erroneously believe that *Adidas* stands for "**A**ll **d**ay, **I** **d**ream **a**bout **s**ports." Not so, though it does stand for something: the name of the company's founder Adolf "**Adi**" **Das**sler.

Other bacronyms were created for serious purposes. For example, although the expression *Amber Alert* originally came from someone's name, that of Amber Hagerman, who was a nine-year-old girl abducted and murdered in 1996, the U.S. Department of Justice defines *Amber Alert* as "**A**merica's **M**issing: **B**roadcast **E**mergency **R**esponse."

EDUCATIONAL BACRONYMS

Many bacronyms are created as mnemonic devices to help people memorize information. Accordingly, the word *Apgar* in *Apgar score*, used to assess the health of newborn babies, has come to be a mnemonic device for "**a**ppearance, **p**ulse, **g**rimace, **a**ctivity, and **p**erspiration." The word was originally simply the last name of

Virginia Apgar, who devised the rating system of newborns. To remember the attributes common to living things, students of biology will think of *MRS. GREN*, which stands for "**m**ovement, **r**espiration, **s**ensitivity, **g**rowth, **r**eproduction, **e**xcretion, and **n**utrition." (For dozens of educational bacronyms, see my *Every Good Boy Deserves Fudge: The Book of Mnemonic Devices*.)

MOTIVATIONAL BACRONYMS

Several bacronyms are popularly used in motivational speeches and literature, including the following:

ACT = **a**ction **c**hanges **t**hings
CARE = **c**hoices, **a**ttitude, **r**esponsibilities, **e**xcellence
FACT = **f**ast **a**ction **c**hanges **t**hings
FEAR = **f**alse **e**ducation **a**ppearing **r**eal
GREAT = **g**et **r**eally **e**xcited **a**bout **t**oday
HOPE = **h**anging **o**nto **p**ositive **e**xpectations
LEAD = **l**earn, **e**ducate, **a**ppreciate, **d**evelop
SMART = **s**pecific, **m**easurable, **a**greed, realistic, **t**imebound (*attributes of effective goals*)
TRUE = **t**rust **r**eleases **u**nbelievable **e**nthusiasm
WIT = **w**hatever **i**t **t**akes

RELIGIOUS BACRONYMS

ACTS = **a**doration, **c**ontrition, **t**hanksgiving, **s**upplication
BIBLE = **b**asic **i**nstructions **b**efore **l**eaving **E**arth
EGO = **e**dging **G**od **o**ut

PRAY = **p**raise, **r**epent, **a**sk, **y**ield
PUSH = **p**ray **u**ntil **s**omething **h**appens

TWELVE-STEP BACRONYMS

DENIAL = **d**on't **e**ven **n**otice **I** **a**m **l**ying
SLIP = **s**obriety **l**osing **i**ts **p**riority

CHAPTER 5

Dennis and Edna Sinned: Palindromes

A *palindrome* is a word, phrase, sentence, or number that can be read the same way in either direction. The word, from the Greek *palin* (back, again) and *dromos* (running), was coined by seventeenth-century English author and dramatist Ben Jonson. Palindromes originated in ancient times. The person usually credited with inventing palindromes was Sotades of Maroneia (in Thrace), who lived in the third century B.C.E. and who wrote palindromic poetry satirizing his government. Legend has it that Ptolemy II was so angered by Sotades' palindromes that he had Sotades captured, sealed in a chest, and thrown into the sea.

The first palindrome in English is ascribed to John Taylor (1580–1653), who used an acceptable seventeenth-century spelling of *dwell* and an ampersand: "Lewd did I live & evil I did dwel."

Although palindromes are associated with wordplay, they can be used, as by Sotades, for political purposes, as in America when people said "No X in Nixon." Further, palindromic numbers interest mathematicians, who can prove that all numerical palindromes with an even number of digits are divisible by eleven.

In English, it is difficult to find palindromic words with more than seven letters. Longer examples include such common words as *Hannah*, *redder*, *repaper*, and *redivider*.

ONE-WORD PALINDROMES

aibohphobia
alula
Anna
cammac
deleveled
detartrated
dewed
evitative
Hannah
kayak
kinnikinnik
level
madam
Malayalam
minim
murdrum
racecar
radar
redder
redivider
refer
reifier
repaper
reviver
rotator

rotor

sagas

solos

sexes

stats

tenet

terret

(MOSTLY) STANDARD PALINDROMES

A dog! A panic in a pagoda.

A man, a plan, a canal, Panama.

A Santa deified at NASA.

A slut nixes sex in Tulsa.

A Toyota.

Able was I ere I saw Elba.

Ah, Satan sees Natasha.

Are we not drawn onward to new era?

Cain: A maniac.

Campus motto: Bottoms up, Mac.

Dee saw a seed.

Delia and Edna ailed.

Dennis and Edna sinned.

Desserts, I stressed.

Do geese see God?

Doc note: I dissent. A fast never prevents a fatness. I diet on cod.

Don't nod.

Dr. Awkward (*real name of a University of Michigan professor*).

Drat Saddam, a mad dastard.

Draw putrid dirt upward.

Dumb mobs bomb mud.

E. Borgnine drags Dad's gardening robe.

E.T. is opposite.

Egad, an adage.

Egad, no bondage.

Elite Tile.

Emil peed deep lime.

Emil saw a slime.

Emus sail, I assume.

Eva, can I stab bats in a cave?

Evade me, Dave.

Evil I did dwell, lewd did I live.

God lived on no devil dog.

Gold log.

He did, eh?

He stops spots, eh?

I madam, I made radio! So I dared. Am I mad? Am I?

I saw desserts; I'd no lemons; alas, no melon. Distressed was I.

Kay, a red nude, peeped under a yak.

Lager, sir, is regal.

Lee had a heel.

Lem saw I was Mel.

Lepers repel.

Lew, Otto has a hot towel.

Liar trial.

Live evil.

Live not on evil.

Lived on decaf, faced no devil.

Lonely Tylenol.

Ma is a nun, as I am.

Mad dastard, a sad rat—Saddam.

Madam, I'm Adam.

Marge lets Norah see Sharon's telegram.

Murder for a jar of red rum.

Must sell at tallest sum.

My gym taxes sex at my gym.

Name now one man.

Neil A. sees alien.

Never odd or even (*also title of a wordplay book by O. V. Michaelsen*).

Niagara, O roar again.

No, Don.

No lemons, no melon.

No, sir, a war is on.

Norma is as selfless as I am, Ron.

Not New York, Roy went on.

Nurses run.

O, Geronimo, no minor ego.

Ogre, flog a golfer. Go.

Oh, no! Don Ho.

OJ nabs Bob's banjo.

Pals slap.

Panda had nap.

Party booby trap.

Party trap.

Petite *p*.

Pull up if I pull up.

Put it up.

Race fast, safe car.

Rats live on no evil star.

Red rum, sir, is murder.

Reflog a golfer.

Regal lager.

Reno loner.

Reviled did I live, said I, as evil I did deliver.

Rise to vote, sir.

Rococo *r*.

Roy, am I mayor?

Sad, no Hondas.

See referees.

Senile felines.

Sex at noon taxes.

Sex-aware era waxes.

Sir, I soon saw Bob was no Osiris.

So many dynamos!

Solo gigolos.

Some men interpret nine memos.

Splat, I hit Alps.

Step on no pets.

Strap on no parts.

Sums are not set as a test on Erasmus.

Sup not on pus.

T. Eliot nixes sex in toilet.

Tie it.

Tip it.

To last, Carter retracts a lot.

Too hot to hoot.

Top spot.

Tulsa night life: filth, gin, a slut.

Tuna nut.

Was it a car or a cat I saw?

Was it a cat I saw?

Was it Eliot's toilet I saw?

We panic in a pew.

We seven, Eve, sew.

Won't cat lovers revolt? Act now!

Won't lovers revolt now?

Wonton? Not now.

Zeus sees Suez.

A phonetic palindrome is a portion of sound or phrase of speech that is identical or roughly identical when reversed. Some phonetic palindromes must be mechanically reversed by using sound recording equipment or some type of reverse tape effect such as back masking.

crew work/work crew
easy
funny enough
Let Bob tell
new moon
Sorry, Ross
Talk, Scott

WORD-UNIT PALINDROMES

Consider the following sentence. "So patient a doctor to doctor a patient so." When the sentence is read backward, beginning with the last word, *so*, it reads the same as it does forward, a phenomenon known as a word-unit palindrome. That sentence, by the way, is from James A. Lindon and has been published in different sources, including the periodical *Word Ways* (ca. 1970) and in O. V. Michaelsen's *Never Odd or Even: Palindromes, Anagrams, & Other Tricks Words Can Do.*

Consider the next word-unit palindrome created by Lindon and published in Martin Gardner's "Mathematical Games" column (*Scientific American*, August

1970): "You can cage a swallow, can't you, but you can't swallow a cage, can you?"

A famous word-unit palindrome is from Alexandre Dumas's *The Three Musketeers*: "All for one and one for all." Finally, the next two word-unit palindromes are from Lindon and published in Charles C. Bombaugh and Gardner's book *Oddities and Curiosities of Words and Literature*:

King, are you glad you are king?
What! So he is hanged, is he? So what?

INTERLUDE 1

A GEOGRAPHICAL BREAK: WORDPLAY INVOLVING PLACE NAMES

PALINDROMIC PLACE NAMES

Ada (*Ohio; Oklahoma; Minnesota*)

Adaven, Nevada (*note that city and state make up a palindrome*)

Akasaka (*Tokyo, Japan*)

Akka (*Morocco*)

Anahanahana (*Madagascar*)

Anina (*Romania*)

Anna (*Estonia*)

Apapa (*Nigeria*)

Arrawarra (*Australia*)

Assamassa (*Portugal*)

Ateleta (*Italy*)

Eleele (*Hawaii*)

Gadag (*Karnataka, India*)

Gaqag (*China*)

Glenelg (*Australia; Scotland; Maryland*)

Hannah (*Lincolnshire, England; North Dakota; South Dakota*)

Harrah (*Oklahoma; Washington*)

Isakasi (*Albania*)

Janaj (*Albania*)

Kanakanak (*Alaska*)

Kangnak (*North Korea*)

Kinikinik (*Colorado*)

Kivik (*Sweden*)

Laval (*Quebec, Canada*)

Lellel (*Mali*)

Level (*Ohio*)

Neuquén (*Argentina*)

Noxon (*Montana*)

Noyon (*France*)

Okonoko (*West Virginia*)

Qaanaaq (*Greenland*)

Remer (*Minnesota*)

Renner (*South Dakota*)

Ruppur (*Bangladesh*)

Sajas (*France*)

Serres (*Greece*)

Tassat (*France*)

Tubbut (*Australia*)

Ward Draw (*South Dakota*)

Wassamassaw (*South Carolina*)

TAUTOLOGICAL PLACE NAMES

In English, when we add the word *river, lake, desert,* or *mountains* to a place name, we'll sometimes generate tautologies (a needless repetition of a word) because the original meaning of the name already includes the topographical feature. One example is *Sahara Desert* because the word *sahara* comes from the Arabic for "desert," making the place name redundant. Languages other than English, however, sometimes contain place names that are tautological, such as *Fjällfjällen* (Swedish for the "mountain mountains"). The following lists present some more tautological place names.

RIVERS

Connecticut River: Algonquin + English = long tidal river river (*United States*)

Cuyahoga River: a Native American language + English = crooked river river (*Ohio*)

Fishkill Creek: Dutch + English = Fish small waterway small waterway (*New York*)

Hatchie River: Muskogean languages + English = river river (*Mississippi; Tennessee*)

Mississippi River: Algonquin + English = big river river (*United States; Canada*)

Paraguay River: Guarani language + English = great river river (*Brazil; Bolivia; Paraguay; Argentina*)

Rillito River: Spanish + English = little river river (*Arizona*)

MOUNTAINS AND HILLS

Bergeberget: Norwegian = the hill hill (*Norway*)

Brindcliffe Edge: Welsh/English = burning hill hill (*Sheffield, United Kingdom*)

Mount Maunganui: Maori = mount mount big (*New Zealand*)

Picacho Peak: Spanish + English = peak peak (*Arizona*)

ISLANDS

Canvey Island: Anglo-Saxon + English = Cana's island island (*United Kingdom*)

Isle of Sheppey: English + Saxon = island of sheep island (*United Kingdom*)

Lundy Island: Norse + English = puffin island island (*United Kingdom*)

Motutapa Island: Maori + English = island sacred island (*New Zealand*)

Walney Island: Old Norse + English = British island island (*United Kingdom*)

CHAPTER 6

Knowledge Is Knowing That a Tomato Is a Fruit; Wisdom Is Knowing Not to Put It in a Fruit Salad: Paraprosdokians

The word *paraprosdokian* (from the Greek for "beyond expectation") describes a figure of speech in which the latter part of a sentence or phrase is surprising or unexpected, causing the reader or listener to reframe or reinterpret the first part. They are sentences with ambushes. They are ideal for humorous or dramatic effect and have often been used by the funniest authors, comedians, and entertainers, including Woody Allen and Groucho Marx.

Where there's a will, I want to be in it. (*Anonymous*)
I belong to no organized party. I am a Democrat. (*Will Rogers*)
I've had a perfectly wonderful evening, but this wasn't it. (*Groucho Marx*)
Time flies like an arrow, fruit flies like a banana. (*Groucho Marx*)
I want to die peacefully in my sleep like my father, not

screaming and terrified like his passengers. (*Bob Monkhouse*)

A modest man, who has much to be modest about. (*Winston Churchill [of Clement Attlee]*)

If you are going through hell, keep going. (*Winston Churchill*)

There will be a rain dance on Friday, weather permitting. (*Steven Wright*)

Take my wife—please. (*Henny Youngman*)

You can always count on Americans to do the right thing—after they've tried everything else. (*Winston Churchill*)

If at first you don't succeed, don't try skydiving. (*Anonymous*)

Mary had a little lamb; the midwife was surprised. (*Anonymous*)

A journey of a thousand miles begins with a cash advance. (*Anonymous*)

Light travels faster than sound. This is why some people appear bright until you hear them speak. (*Anonymous*)

Two elderly women are at a Catskill Mountain resort, and one of 'em says, "Boy, the food at this place is really terrible." The other one says, "Yeah, I know, and such small portions." (*Woody Allen*)

Outside of a dog, a book is a man's best friend. Inside of a dog, it's too dark to read. (*Groucho Marx*)

I decided to go on a draconian diet, cutting alcohol, fat, and sugar. In two weeks, I lost fourteen days. (*Tim Maia*)

We broke up because I saw her lying—under another man. (*Doug Benson*)

If I am reading this graph correctly—I would be very surprised. (*Stephen Colbert*)

If only I could see a miracle, like a burning bush, or the seas part, or my Uncle Sasha pick up a check! (*Woody Allen [in the film* Love and Death*]*)

The car stopped on a dime, which unfortunately was in a pedestrian's pocket. (*Anonymous*)

The coffee is good to the last drop. What happened to the last drop I'll never know. (*Anonymous*)

I once shot an elephant in my pajamas. How he got in my pajamas I don't know. (*Groucho Marx*)

I asked God for a bike, but I know God doesn't work that way. So I stole the bike and asked for forgiveness. (*Anonymous*)

A bus station is where a bus stops. A train station is where a train stops. On my desk, I have a work station. (*Anonymous*)

How is it one careless match can start a forest fire, but it takes a whole box to start a campfire? (*Anonymous*)

Why do Americans choose from just two people to run for president and fifty for Miss America? (*Anonymous*)

You do not need a parachute to skydive. You only need a parachute to skydive twice. (*Anonymous*)

Change is inevitable, except from a vending machine. (*Anonymous*)

CHAPTER 7

Meet Fred Derf: Semordnilaps

When a word such as *rotator* can be spelled the same forward and backward, it's a palindrome. When a word spelled backward, such as *pots*, yields another word (*stop*), it's a semordnilap, which is *palindromes* spelled backward. Although the underlying concept of a semordnilap can be found at least as far back as Lewis Carroll's novel *Sylvie and Bruno* (1889), Carroll didn't use the term. The founder of the recreational linguistics journal *Word Ways*, Dmitri Borgmann, was either the first person to use the term *semordnilap* or was among the first. By the way, the longest common English semordnilap is probably *desserts/stressed*.

A number of semordnilaps follow.

bag	gab
ban	nab
bard	drab
bat	tab
bats	stab
bed	Deb/deb (*debutante*)

bid	dib
bin	nib
blub	bulb
bog	gob
bonk	knob
boy	yob
brag	garb
bro	orb
bud	dub
bun	nub
buns	snub
bur (*variation of burr*)	rub
bus	sub
but	tub
buts	stub
cam	mac
cap	PAC (*political action committee*)
caw	WAC (*Women's Army Corps*)
cram	Marc
dag	gad
dam	mad
Damon	nomad
dart	trad (*traditional; British*)
decaf	faced
decal	laced

deem	meed
deep	peed
deer	reed
deifier	reified
Deiter	retied
Delbert	trebled
Delians (*those from Delos*)	snailed
deliver	reviled
demit	timed
den	Ned
denier	reined
denim	mined
Dennis	sinned
depot	toped
dessert	tressed
desserts	stressed
devil	lived
dew	wed
dial	laid
diaper	repaid
dig	gid
dim	mid
dine	Enid
dioramas	samaroid
do	od
don	nod
doom	mood

door	rood
DOS/dos	sod
draw	ward
drawer	reward
draws	sward
dray	yard
dual	laud
dub	bud
Edam	made
edit	tide
eel	lee
eh	he
Elbert	treble
Ellen	Nelle
em	me
Emil	lime
emit	time
er	re
Eris	sire
Eros	sore
Eton	note
evil	live
gnat	tang
gnaw	Wang
gnus	sung
got	tog
gulp	plug

gums	smug
guns	snug
gut	tug
haiku	Ukiah
hales	selah
Harpo	Oprah
it	ti
keel	leek
keels	sleek
keep	peek
jar	raj/Raj
Kay	yak
knaps	spank
knits	stink
knob	bonk
know	wonk
K.O.	O.K.
Kool	look
lager	regal
lair	rial
lap	pal
leer	reel
Leon	Noel/noel
leper	repel
leveler	relevel
lever	revel
liar	rail

lien	Neil
loop	pool
loops	spool
loot	tool
looter	retool
loots	stool
map	Pam
maps	spam
mar	ram
mart	tram
mat	tam
maws	swam
may	yam
meet	teem
Mets	stem
moor	room
mot	Tom/tom
namer	reman
nap	pan
naps	span
natures	Serutan (*laxative*)
Nemo	omen
net	ten
nip	pin
nips	spin
nit	tin
no	on

nor	Ron
not	ton
note	Eton
notes	Seton
now	won
nuts	stun
oat	Tao
ohm	mho
oohs	shoo
os	so
oy	yo
pacer	recap
pals	slap
pans	snap
par	rap
part	trap
parts	strap
pas	sap
pat	tap
paws	swap
pay	yap
peels	sleep
pees	seep
per	rep
pets	step
pins	snip
pit	tip

pools	sloop
ports	strop
pot	top
pots	stop
prat	tarp
pus	sup
raps	spar
rat	tar
rats	star
raw	war
rebut	tuber
redraw	warder
redrawer	rewarder
reknit	tinker
reknits	stinker
remit	timer
rennet	tenner
repot	toper
rot	tor
saps	spas
saved	Vedas
saw	was
sew	Wes
sloops	spools
smart	trams
smut	Tums (*antacid*)
snaps	spans

snips	spins
snoops	spoons
snoot	toons
snot	tons
spat	taps
spay	yaps
spit	tips
sports	strops
spot	tops
spots	stops
sprat	tarps
stat	tats
stows	swots
straw	warts
Suez	Zeus
sway	yaws
swot	tows
tort	trot
tow	wot
way	yaw

CHAPTER 8

Socrates Was the Wisest Athenian Because He Alone Knew That He Was Ignorant: Paradoxical Statements

A paradox is a seemingly true statement or group of statements leading to a contradiction or a situation that defies logic or intuition. Many paradoxical statements don't imply a logical contradiction but seem to run counter to what many people believe. For example, it may seem false, but it is sound psychology to realize that the best way to impress people is to show that one is impressed by them. Other paradoxical statements may rely on wordplay or ambiguity, as when someone argues that the soul is immaterial, that immaterial things are unimportant, and that the soul is therefore unimportant.

There are also logical paradoxes. Consider the barber paradox, popularized by Bertrand Russell. Suppose that there is a town with just one male barber who shaves all and only those men who don't shave themselves.

Everything seems logical until we ask, Who shaves the barber? If we say the barber shaves himself, we contradict the original conditions, which say that he shaves only those men who don't shave themselves. If the barber doesn't shave himself, that hypothesis also contradicts the original conditions, which say that the barber shaves all those men who don't shave themselves. In short, the barber in the barber paradox must both shave and not shave himself—a self-contradictory state of affairs. Although whole books have been written on paradoxes, we can here content ourselves with recognizing that the barber in the paradox can't (logically) exist because his description is self-contradictory.

The following paradoxical statements are insightful, but there aren't, strictly speaking, logical paradoxes:

Real knowledge is to know the extent of one's ignorance. (*Confucius*)

That saying is reminiscent of Socrates, who said that he was the wisest man in all Athens because he alone knew that he was ignorant.

People have one thing in common: they are all different. (*Robert Zend*)

The most incomprehensible thing about the world is that it is comprehensible. (*Albert Einstein*)

Sometimes you have to be silent to be heard. (*Stanislaw Lec*)

Silence is unbearable repartee. (*G. K. Chesterton*)

The exit is usually where the entrance was. (*Stanislaw Lec*)

The way up is also the way down. (*Heraclitus*)

On every summit you are on the brink of an abyss. (*Stanislaw Lec*)

Often it is fatal to live too long. (*Racine*)

I have made this letter longer than usual because I lacked the time to make it shorter. (*Pascal*)

I must follow the people. Am I not their leader? (*Benjamin Disraeli*)

Don't vote. The government will get in. (*an anarchist*)

We are tomorrow's past. (*Mary Webb*)

A mask tells us more than a face. (*Oscar Wilde*)

Tact consists in knowing how far to go too far. (*Jean Cocteau*)

Dear God: I know you will provide, but why don't you provide *until* you provide? (*Leo Rosten; a Jewish saying*)

CHAPTER 9

Meet the New Guest Host: Oxymora

An oxymoron is an expression that contains words or elements with opposite meanings, as in *guest host*. Just as the word *bittersweet* is oxymoronic, so the word *oxymoronic* contains self-contradictory elements—*oxys* (sharp, keen) and *moros* (foolish), yielding "pointedly foolish." The word *sophomoric* is literally "a wise fool" because such a student hasn't the complete foolishness of a freshman or the complete wisdom of a senior. *Preposterous* is literally "pertaining to before-after." What's more, *cosmopolitan* is literally a "citizen of the world."

Oxymora can be classified in different ways; the typology used here is useful.

SINGLE-WORD OXYMORA COMPOSED OF ANTAGONISTIC ELEMENTS

As we've seen sophomores are "wise fools" (or pointedly foolish) and preposterous things are "before-after." A term from music is *pianoforte* (the original name of a piano), literally "soft-loud."

SINGLE-WORD OXYMORA COMPOSED OF INDEPENDENT MORPHEMES

Some oxymoronic words contain two morphemes (meaning-bearing elements), each of which could qualify as a word in itself. Accordingly, we have *bridegroom* (bride + groom), *bittersweet* (bitter + sweet), and *ballpoint* (ball + point).

LITERAL OXYMORA

Some oxymora don't require plays on words or personal values or points of view (such as *military intelligence*) but rather are evident contradictions when people consider the literal meanings of their component words.

benevolent despot
benign neglect
current history
drive-in exit
dry lake
elevated subway
fresh frozen
ivory black
living end
loyal opposition
one-man band

open secret
original copy
preventive medicine
random order
turn up missing
working vacation

PUN-BASED OXYMORA

Perhaps the best-known oxymoron in the United States was made popular by word-loving comedian George Carlin: *jumbo shrimp*. The phrase can be treated as an oxymoron because the word *shrimp* is sometimes used to describe not a decapod crustacean but something small for its kind, as when bullies threaten to pick on kids they call "shrimps." Other examples of pun-based oxymora are *even odds* and *death benefit*.

PARTS OF SPEECH

Some expressions can be treated as oxymora when their components are treated as one part of speech rather than another. The following expressions become oxymoronic when their component words are treated as verbs rather than as nouns: *press release*, *divorce court*, and *building wrecking*.

DEAD METAPHORS

A word can lose its original meaning and become a vague expression of positive or negative emotion or an expression of degree (*fairly*). Sometimes enough of the original meaning of a word exists to create tension with the word with which it is paired. *Fabulous* no longer denotes "based on a fable," and *awful* no longer means "awe-inspiring." Examples of oxymora based on dead metaphors include *awful(ly) good*, *damned good*, *barely clothed*, and *clearly confusing*.

ARTFUL OXYMORA

Some oxymora reflect conscious contrivance, as when Stephen Douglas was dubbed the "Little Giant." Other examples are *same difference*, *global village*, and *accidentally on purpose*.

LITERARY OXYMORA

Stark oxymoronic language is skillfully used by many great writers. Some examples:

bookful blockhead ignorantly read (*Pope*)
concord of this discord (*Shakespeare*)
damn with faint praise (*Pope*)
darkness visible (*Milton*)
falsely true (*Tennyson*)
fearful bravery (*Shakespeare*)
hateful good (*Chaucer*)
loving hate (*Shakespeare*)
miserable abundance (*Donne*)

DOUBLESPEAK OXYMORA

Sometimes—especially in politics or advertising—oxymora are created to mislead or confuse, such as *mandatory option* and *virtually spotless.*

PARTISAN OXYMORA

When people project their values into interpretations of language, expressions not usually intended as oxymora can be interpreted ironically and indeed oxymoronically. The following expressions, when used cynically or comically (as by professional comedians), express points of view that either will resonate with people and possibly entertain them or will alienate them.

George Carlin and other comedians have held that these expressions are oxymoronic:

business ethics
educational television
military intelligence
moral majority
nonworking mother
postal service
student athlete
young Republican

TECHNOLOGICAL INNOVATIONS

Some phrases that are literally oxymoronic were created because of emerging technologies, such as *paper*

OXYMORONIC STATEMENTS

Never say never.
Avoid clichés like the plague.
If I did say that, I was misquoted.
I'd give my right arm to be ambidextrous.
When you fall and break both your legs, don't come
     running to me.
If you don't get this note, let me know immediately.
I pride myself on my humility.

---

tablecloths, *metalwood*, *plastic glasses*, *green black-board*, and *plastic silverware*.

The following list of oxymora was gleaned from numerous sources:

adult children
advanced BASIC
almost safe
artificial grass
assistant principal
baby giant
backside
bigger half
big town
bland spice
blind sight
calm storm
career criminal

career gambler

care industry

clean coal

coal mine safety

common royalty

communist respect for the individual

compassionate dictator

deciding not to decide

down escalator

drink oneself sober

elevated subway

final draft

free with purchase

full of holes (*no object could be completely holey*)

Good grief!

Greece's fiscal responsibility

historical fiction

holy war

lay professional

modern classic

negative growth

numb feeling

rolling stop

science fiction

shortless and shoeless, with trousers to match

sight unseen

CHAPTER 10

When Words Sound Like Letters: Alphabet Words

When you recite the alphabet, you are reciting not only the letters of the alphabet but also at least one identically pronounced word for each letter. We call those words alphabet words. Although it is easy to find one word pronounced like any given letter, it is more difficult to find two words that are pronounced the same. Occasionally, one can find three words pronounced like one letter, as in *be*, *Bea*, and *bee*.

A = a
B = be, Bea, bee
C = see, sea
D = dee (*an electrode in a cyclotron*), Dee
E = ee (*Scottish for "eye"*)
F = eff (*a lizard-like animal, usually referred to as a newt*)
G = Gee!
H = aitch-bone (*the rump of beef*)
I = eye, aye
J = jay (*bluejay or jaybird*)
K = cay (*a small, low island*)
L = ell

M = em (*a printer's measure*)
N = en (*a printer's measure*)
O = owe, oh
P = pea, pee
Q = cue, queue
R = are
S = ess
T = tea, tee
U = ewe, you
V = vee
W = double you (*a betting expression*)
X = ex
Y = why
Z = z-bar

CHAPTER 11

Making Every Letter Count: Pangrams

A pangram (Greek: *pan gramma*) is a holoalphabetic sentence—that is, a sentence that uses every letter of the alphabet at least once. Although pangrams are examples of wordplay, they are used to display typefaces; test equipment; and develop skills in handwriting, keyboarding, and calligraphy. The most famous English pangram, "The quick brown fox jumps over the lazy dog," was used by Western Union to test Telex/TWX data communication equipment for accuracy and reliability and is now used by some computer programs to display computer fonts.

A perfect pangram in the English language will contain every letter of the alphabet only once and will be incomprehensible to almost everybody but word mavens. A common example of a perfect English pangram is "Cwm fjord-bank glyphs vext quiz," roughly equivalent to "Carved symbols in a mountain hollow on the bank of an inlet irritated an eccentric person."

Imperfect pangrams, in which one or more letters are repeated, are easier to understand and more likely to make sense. Consider the following pangrams, some of which are more meaningful than others:

Pack my box with five dozen liquor jugs.

The five boxing wizards jump quickly.

Glib jocks quiz nymphs to vex dwarf.

A quick blowing zephyr vexes bold Jim.

Sex-charged fop blew my junk TV quiz.

Two driven jocks help fax my big quiz.

Blowzy red vixens fight for a quick jump.

GQ jock wears vinyl tuxedo for show-biz promo.

Pack my red box with five dozen quality jugs.

Watch *Jeopardy!*, Alex Trebek's fun TV quiz game.

Sexy prof gives back no quiz with mild joy.

Fax back Jim's Gwyneth Paltrow video quiz.

Amazingly few discotheques provide jukeboxes.

Sympathizing would fix Quaker objectives.

CHAPTER 12

Livia Soprano Is an Albacore around Johnny Soprano's Neck: Malapropisms

The word *malapropism* comes from the name of the character Mrs. Malaprop, who appears in Richard Sheridan's play *The Rivals* and who would often mistake words for words that sounded like them, as when she said *allegory* for *alligator*. A malapropism occurs when (1) a word or phrase that is used means something different from what was intended, (2) the word or phrase sounds at least somewhat like the intended word or phrase, (3) the word or phrase that is used has a recognized meaning in the user's language, and (4) the resulting language is nonsense or something close to it. Consequently, although the verb *jive* (to play or dance to jive music; to chat; to talk nonsense or to kid) can qualify as a malapropism for the similar-sounding verb *jibe* (to be in accord with), the word *acute* can't qualify as a malapropism for the word *abstruse* because they don't sound alike.

THE FUNNIEST CAMPAIGN SPEECH THAT
GEORGE SMATHERS NEVER GAVE

Although George Smathers attacked the then-incumbent U.S. senator Claude Pepper in the Democratic senatorial primary in 1950 as having communist sympathies, that race is famous or infamous for a funny speech that Smathers was alleged to have given but never gave. A reporter's hoax had it that Smathers gave a speech to a rural audience using fancy words that sounded negative but weren't negative, except perhaps for *nepotism*. According to the ruse, Smathers said:

> *Are you aware that Claude Pepper is known all over Washington as a shameless extrovert? Not only that, but this man is reliably reported to practice nepotism with his sister-in-law, and he has a sister who was once a thespian in wicked New York. Worst of all, it is an established fact that Mr. Pepper before his marriage habitually practiced celibacy.*

COMMON MALAPROPISMS

bare [*bear*] in mind
child progeny [*prodigy*]
civil serpent [*servant*]
complete forest [*farce*]
D. H. Lawrence's erratic [*erotic*] writing
"Don't" is a contraption [*contraction*]
extra-century [*extra-sensory*] perception
fire distinguisher [*extinguisher*]

game was a cliff-dweller [*cliff-hanger*]

ginkgo balboa [*biloba*]

had to evaporate [*evacuate*] the neighborhood

hostile remarks exasperated [*exacerbated*] the situation

plans didn't jive [*jibe*] with mine

man of great statue [*stature*]

neutrons [*croutons*] in the salad

pacific [*specific*] example

pendulum [*pendant*] around her neck

pigment [*figment*] of the imagination

points I eluded [*alluded*] to

popular [*poplar*] trees

sixteenth [*Sistine*] chapel

statue [*statute*] of limitations

was given an old tomato [*ultimatum*]: adjust or leave

MALAPROPISMS IN MISTRANSLATIONS

It is often more convenient and less expensive to buy language-translating software than to hire a professional translator who is well versed in the language in question. Thus merchants catering to tourists often count on software, unaware of the program's inability to capture English idioms, vocabulary, and syntax. To appreciate how difficult it can be to understand a foreign language, consider that the meaning of words and phrases are sometimes context specific. For example, in English, as Richard Lederer has cleverly observed, we go to the bathroom in order to go to the bathroom.

The following mistranslations were gathered from websites that record English-language signs spotted in non-English-speaking countries throughout the world.

Every mistranslation is an unintentional pun, double entendre, or malapropism.

The manager has personally passed all the water served here. (*Acapulco, hotel*)

Visitors are expected to complain at the office between the hours of 9 and 11 A.M. daily. (*Athens, hotel*)

It is forbidden to enter a woman even a foreigner if dressed as a man. (*Bangkok, temple*)

The lift is being fixed for the next day. During that time we regret that you will be unbearable. (*Bucharest, hotel*)

Teeth extracted by the latest Methodists. (*Hong Kong, ad*)

For your convenience, we recommend courteous, efficient self-service. (*Hong Kong, supermarket*)

Ladies may have a fit upstairs. (*Hong Kong, tailor shop*)

We take your bags and send them in all directions. (*Copenhagen, airport*)

To stop the drip, turn cock to right. (*Finland, washroom*)

You are invited to take advantage of the chambermaid. (*Japan, hotel*)

Please leave your values at the front desk. (*Paris, hotel*)

Specialist in women and other diseases. (*Rome, doctor's office*)

Our wines leave you nothing to hope for. (*Switzerland, menu*)

Because of the impropriety of entertaining guests of the opposite sex in the bedroom, it is suggested that the lobby be used for this purpose. (*Zurich, hotel*)

Would you like to ride on your own ass? (*Thailand, ad*)

Special cocktails for the ladies with nuts. (*Tokyo, bar*)

ROD L. EVANS

INTERLUDE 2

AN ATHLETIC BREAK: WORDPLAY INVOLVING SPORTS FIGURES' MALAPROPISMS AND UNUSUAL NAMES IN SPORTS

MALAPROPISMS, ABSURDITIES, OR CRAZY PUNS FROM SPORTS FIGURES

YOGI BERRA

"It gets late early out here."

"The future ain't what it used to be."

"Never answer an anonymous letter."

"It's like déjà vu all over again."

"He hits from both side of the plate. He's amphibious."

When asked about his choice of burial sites: "Surprise me."

MIKE TYSON

When asked about his retirement plans: "Fade into Bolivian, I guess."

JOE THEISMANN

"The term 'genius' is inapplicable to anyone in this game. A genius is Norman Einstein."

GEORGE FOREMAN

"There's more to boxing than hitting. There's not getting hit, for instance."

DIZZY DEAN (FROM WWW.DIZZYDEAN.COM)

"The doctors X-rayed my head and found nothing."

"He slud into third."

"The good Lord was good to me. He gave me a strong body, a good right arm, and a weak mind."

TUG MCGRAW

When asked whether he preferred grass or AstroTurf, "I dunno. I never smoked AstroTurf."

"Always root for the winner. That way you won't be disappointed."

GEORGE ROBERTS

"I want to rush for 1,000 or 1,500 yards, whichever comes first."

BOBBY HOYING

On his Ohio State team: "I'm really happy for Coach Cooper and the guys who have been here six or seven years, especially our seniors."

RON MEYER

On the chances of leading the Colts to the Promised Land: "It's not like we came down from Mount Sinai with the tabloids."

BILL COWHER

On whether the Steelers bent NFL regulations: "We're not attempting to circumcise the rules."

ANDRE DAWSON

On the need to be a role model: "I want all the kids to copulate me."

PEDRO GUERRERO

On the press: "Sometimes they write what I say, not what I mean."

MIKE GREENWELL

"I'm just a four-wheel-drive pickup kind of guy, and so's my wife."

MARVIN "BAD NEWS" BARNES

When told his flight would depart at 9 a.m. EST and arrive at 8:59 a.m. CST: "I don't know about you, but I ain't gettin' in no time machine."

LOU DUVA

"You can sum up this sport [boxing] in two words, you never know."

CHUCK NEVITT

On why he seemed nervous: "My sister is having a baby, and I don't know if I'm going to be an aunt or an uncle."

DON KING

"He [Chávez] speaks English, Spanish, and he's bilingual."

MOST ENTERTAINING NAMES IN SPORTS

Albert Pujols (*St. Louis Cardinals*)

Assoli Slivets (*Olympia freestyle skier*)

Boof Bonser (*New York Mets and other teams*)

Chief Kickingstallionsims (*Alabama State basketball team*)

Coco Crisp (*Oakland Athletics and other teams*)

Craphonso Thorpe (*Florida State football team and NFL teams*)

Fat Lever (*Denver Nuggets*)

God Shammgod (*Portland Chinooks*)

Harry Colon (*New England Patriots and other teams*)

Homer Bush (*New York Yankees*)

I. M. Hipp (*Nebraska football team*)

John Arthur "Chubby" Cox (*University of San Francisco basketball team and NBA teams*)

John Wesley "Jack" Glasscock (*MLB teams*)

Longar Longar (*Oklahoma basketball team*)

Luscious Pusey (*Eastern Illinois football team*)

Milton Bradley (*MLB teams*)

Misty Hyman (*Olympic butterfly swimmer*)

Peter LaCock (*Chicago Cubs and Kansas City Royals*)

Razor Shines (*New York Mets*)

Richard "Dick" Trickle (*race car driver*)

Ron Tugnutt (*Quebec Nordiques*)

Rusty Kuntz (*Minnesota Twins*)

Shadow Pyle (*Philadelphia Quakers*)

Tony Suck (*born Charles Anthony Zuck; MLB*)

"Ugly" Johnny Dickshot (*Pittsburgh Pirates and other teams*)

Urban Shocker (*born Urban Jacques Shocker; New York Yankees and St. Louis Braves*)

Van Lingle Mungo (*Brooklyn Dodgers*)

Wonderful Terrific Monds II (*Atlanta Braves*)

World B. Free (*born Lloyd Bernard Free; NBA teams*)

CHAPTER 13

President Reagan Succumbed to Old-Timer's Disease: Eggcorns

The term *eggcorn* was coined by Geoffrey Pullum in September 2003 in response to a post by Mark Liberman on the blog *Language Log*. Liberman wrote that there is no term for the mistake of substituting the phrase *eggcorn* or *egg corn* for *acorn*. Pullum suggested using *eggcorn* itself.

An eggcorn is an idiosyncratic substitution of a word or phrase for a word or phrase that sounds similar or the same in the speaker's dialect. The resulting new word or phrase, though different from the original, exhibits logic or creativity, producing a phrase that may be (often unintentionally) insightful or may lead to an insightful interpretation of what was originally described. Although classical malapropisms are normally funny and produce nonsense or something approaching it, eggcorns have an underlying logic. The relevant connection (albeit tenuous) between eggs and acorns is their shapes.

To see why using *eggcorn* to describe the phenomenon may not be the best term (though I have no replacement), consider an excellent example of the phenomenon—calling Alzheimer's disease *old-timer's disease*. Because the incidence of Alzheimer's disease increases with age, the substitution is appropriate. Another good example of an eggcorn is the use of *mating name* for *maiden name*. Eggcorns often involve replacing an unfamiliar, archaic, or obscure word with a more common or modern word, as when people write *baited breath* for *bated breath*.

A FUNNY EGGCORN FROM MANGLING SHAKESPEARE

A particularly creative eggcorn occurs when a person says that someone was "hoist with his own canard" for "hoist with his own petard" ("to be harmed by one's own plan to harm someone else"). The expression with the word *petard* was made famous by Shakespeare's *Hamlet*, act III, scene 4, lines 206 and 207: "For 'tis the sport to have the engineer / Hoist with his own petar [*sic*]." Hamlet is chuckling over the fate he has in store for Rosencrantz and Guildenstern, who are plotting to have him killed. Hamlet turns their plot against them by substituting their names for his in the death warrant they carry from King Claudius. He continues: "But I will delve one yard below their mines / And blow them at the moon." The word *mines*, as in "land mines," describes a bomb—that is, a small explosive device designed to blow open barricaded doors and gates. A petard, or, in Shakespeare's spelling, "petar," is a bomb. Hamlet was saying, metaphorically, that he would bury his bomb beneath Rosencrantz and Guildenstern and "hoist" them ("blow them at the moon"). Although Hamlet was protecting his life and so wasn't farting around, the word *petard* comes from Middle French *peter*, which derives in turn from the Latin *peditum*, the neuter of *peditus*, past participle of *pedere* (to break wind). Now back to the relevant eggcorn. Because a canard is a deliberately misleading fabrication, "to hoist with one's own canard" can describe a situation in which a lie turns against the liar.

Because the line between malapropism and eggcorn can't always be drawn with mathematical precision, some people can reasonably disagree over whether some phrase is one or the other. What follows is a list of expressions that many people would say qualify as eggcorns.

a hare's [*hair's*] breadth
a mute [*moot*] point
a pigment [*figment*] of my imagination
above / beyond approach [*reproach*]
all for knot [*naught*]
all goes [*augurs*] well
anchors away [*aweigh*]
baited [*bated*] breath
balling [*bawling*] one's eyes out
bare [*bear*] the brunt
bear-faced [*barefaced*] lie
bear-knuckled [*bare-knuckled*]
beckon [*begging*] the question

A DIALOGUE BETWEEN MR. EGGCORN MALAPROP
(A POLITICIAN) AND A JOURNALIST

Journalist: You've said that corporations are destroying this country. What did you mean?

Mr. Eggcorn Malaprop: Corporations are too influential in determining public policy and our future. Most of us Americans are just prawns in a giant game of chest.

Journalist: You claim that corporations are stealing from the poor and that the wealthiest 10 percent of income earners pay no taxes. Are you aware that the bottom 47 percent of income earners pay no federal income tax, and many of them get money from other taxpayers in the form of earned income tax credits? Further, the top 10 percent of wage earners pay a disproportionately large percentage of federal income taxes.

Mr. Eggcorn Malaprop: You're taking me out of contest. You're attacking my self-of-steam! Rich people are rich because they prey on the poor.

Journalist: Do you have any statistics from legitimate sources, including reputable news magazines? Do you know exact statistics on what different groups of taxpayers pay in taxes?

Mr. Eggcorn Malaprop: I can't afford a lot of magazine prescriptions, and I don't have a photogenic memory. I just want the income tax code to be fair. We need to let the Bush tax cuts relapse. I'll have you know that I may not be a bookworm, but I get a lot of information from my wife, who is a college grad and one with woman's intermission.

Journalist: Do you think that Republicans who argue that removing the tax cuts will hurt the economy are fallacious in their thinking?

Mr. Eggcorn Malaprop: Look, I don't care what they do in private. All I know is that the unions used to be strong in the 1960s, when we had an effluent society. Look at the unemployment rate; look at outsourcing.

Journalist: Yes, some things are worse now than they were in the 1960s. But look at all the consumer choices; we've never had such a large variety of potato chips and orange juice.

Mr. Eggcorn Malaprop: I don't care about low-Hassidic orange juice! I want to see more jobs and lower prices.

Journalist: Do you think that we need a bigger stimulus package?

Mr. Eggcorn Malaprop: Yes, rich people are taking their status for granite. We need more Democrats so that the government can take care of us when we retire.

Journalist: Do you think that Republicans don't care about the elderly?

Mr. Eggcorn Malaprop: Of course they don't. They want most people to die as soon as they retire to reduce Medicare costs. It was mostly the Democrats who gave us Medicare. It's the Democrats who'll be there when we get old-timer's disease. The Republicans don't want to help the poor and elderly, but they have trillions for wars and the pentagram. Sorry. I've got to go. Some of us have real jobs.

beckon call [*beck and call*]

beyond the pail [*pale*]

blessing from the skies [*blessing in disguise*]

boggled [*bogged*] down

bonified [*bona fide*]

bread [*bed*] and breakfast

buck [*butt*] of jokes

buttkiss [*bubkes, bupkis, bupkes, bupkus*]

cast dispersions [*aspersions*]

cliff-dweller [*cliff-hanger*]

curled up in the feeble [*fetal*] position

cyberstocking [*cyberstalking*]

deformation [*defamation*] of character

dire rear [*diarrhea*]

doggy-dog [*dog-eat-dog*]

draw a beat [*bead*] on

due [*do*] or die

dull drums [*doldrums*]

enact [*exact*] revenge

ex-patriot [*expatriate*]

expresso [*espresso*]

exuberant [*exorbitant*] prices

far-gone [*foregone*] conclusion

fast [*vast*] majority

floorless [*flawless*] display of agility

flush [*flesh*] out

font [*fount*] of wisdom

for all intensive [*intents and*] purposes

forward [*foreword*]

free reign [*rein*]

fullproof [*foolproof*]

furled [*furrowed*] brow

gamefully [*gainfully*] employed

garbledygood [*gobbledygook*]

get one's dandruff [*dander*] up
getting the load down [*low-down*]
go at it hammer and thongs [*tongs*]
in lame man's [*layman's*] terms
lip-sing [*lip-sync*]
preying mantis [*praying mantis*]
shoe-in [*shoo-in*]
wet [*whet*] one's appetite
without further to do [*ado*]

CHAPTER 14

I Scream for Ice Cream: Oronyms

An oronym is a string of words or a phrase that sounds the same as another string of words or phrase but is spelled differently, such as *ice cream* and *I scream*. The

---

IOWANS LOVED TO SEE FONDA DICKS SCORE, BUT AUTHORS STILL LOVE THE SERVICES OF PENNY HOARE

Oronyms, as we've seen, are phrases that are accidentally homophonic with other phrases. Sometimes people's names sound the same as expressions that are risqué or outrageous. On December 12, 1972, Fonda Dicks, basketball superstar for the Moravia High Mohawkettes in Moravia, Iowa, scored 64 points against Seymour High, which scored only 56 points. She was the female Michael Jordan at Moravia High, but with a name much more amusing. As to Penny Hoare, she's a well-known book editor in England whose first name, Penelope, is inevitably shortened to Penny.

term was coined by Gyles Brandreth and first published in his classic book *The Joy of Lex*.

The comedian Jeff Foxworthy often uses oronyms in his Appalachian comedy routine, as when he uses a sentence with *moustache*: "I moustache [must ask] you a question."

It occurred on a sadder day [*Saturday*].
I can hear the night train [*rain*].
She took a nice [*an ice-*] cold shower.
Some others [*mothers*] I've known are there.
Don't pinch her ear [*rear*].
The stuffy nose [*stuff he knows*] can be disturbing.
The sons raise meat [*sun's rays meet*].
She liked her new toy Yoda [*Toyota*].

CHAPTER 15

How to Turn "Revved Up Like a Deuce" into "Wrapped Up Like a Douche": Mondegreens

A mondegreen has been called an aural malapropism, a mishearing of a word or phrase in such a way as to give it a new meaning. The term was coined by writer Sylvia Wright in a 1954 essay for *Harper's Magazine*. As a child, Wright heard the Scottish ballad "The Bonny Earl of Murray" and misheard and thus misinterpreted the last few words of the following stanza:

Ye Highlands and ye Lowlands,
Oh, where hae ye been?
They hae skin the Earl O' Murray,
And laid him on the green.

For years Wright believed that the line "And laid him on the green" was "And Lady Mondegreen." How touching, she thought, for a tragic heroine to die with her liege. Only years later did Wright discover that

Lady Mondegreen was not killed with Earl O' Murray. So distraught was Wright by the disappearance of her personal imaginary heroine that she memorialized Lady Mondegreen with a neologism.

Covers of songs can contain mondegreens. For example, when Joan Baez covered the song "The Night They Drove Old Dixie Down," originally recorded in 1969 by the Band, she changed the occupation of the narrator, Virgil Caine, from a farmer to that of a laborer with the words, "Like my father before me, I'm a working man." The original lyrics were "Like my father before me, I will work the land." Baez later admitted that she sang it the way she had heard it and had never seen the printed lyrics before she sang it. There are other mondegreens in that song, as when Baez sings "the blood below my feet" instead of the original "the mud below my feet."

THE REASON FOR THIS CHAPTER'S TITLE

One of rock's most popular mondegreens is a lyric in "Blinded by the Light," a cover of a Bruce Springsteen song by Manfred Mann's Earth Band. Millions of listeners would probably bet money that they hear the words "wrapped up like a douche" when the actual words are supposed to be "revved up like a deuce," as in a deuce coupe.

BOB DYLAN, MARIJUANA, AND "I WANT TO HOLD YOUR HAND"

When Bob Dylan offered marijuana to the Beatles, he was surprised that they had not tried it before; he had misheard the lyric "I can't hide" in "I Want to Hold Your Hand" as "I get high," which was part of a lyric in another famous Beatles song.

JONI MITCHELL AND A. GRAHAM BELL

In Joni Mitchell's cover of the Lambert, Hendricks & Ross song "Twisted," she changes the original lyric "they all laughed at A. Graham Bell" to "they all laugh at angry young men."

"MAIRZY DOATS"

"Mairzy Doats" is a novelty song composed in 1943 that made the pop charts several times and was a hit for the quartet the Merry Macs. The song is based on an English nursery rhyme, which includes some mondegreens and their corrections. Its refrain seems meaningless:

Mairzy doats and dozy doats and liddle lamzy divey
A kiddley divey, too, wouldn't you? [pronounced *wooden shoe*]

The lyrics of the bridge, however, provide a clue:

*If the words sound queer and funny to your ear, a
   little bit jumbled and jivey
Sing "Mares eat oats and does eat oats and little
   lambs eat ivy."*

With that aid, the refrain becomes more easily understood, and the ear can detect the hidden message of the final line:

A kid'll eat ivy too, wouldn't you?

NONMUSICAL MONDEGREENS

Although most mondegreens people discuss are from songs, mondegreens can be inspired by other language, as in the Pledge of Allegiance, as when people "pledge a lesion to the flag . . . and to the republic for Richard Stans . . . with liver tea and justice for all," and when people recite The Lord's Prayer and say "Our Father, Who art in Heaven, Harold be thy name." In fact, one of the best-known mondegreens is inspired by the phrase "lead us not into temptation" in The Lord's Prayer, which has sometimes been recited by children as "lead us not into Penn Station."

As author Sylvia Wright illustrated by her creating the word *mondegreen*, mondegreens can be inspired by literature. In fact, the title of J. D. Salinger's *The Catcher in the Rye* comes from the protagonist Holden Caulfield's mishearing a sung version of Robert Burns's poem "Coming through the Rye": the line "Gin a body meet a body / Comin thro' the rye" is misunderstood

by Holden as "Gin a body catch a body / Comin thro'
the rye."

THE MOST FRIGHTENING
MONDEGREEN

A leading nutritionist on *Good Morning America* was
heard (or misheard) as saying, "The average American will gain forty-seven pounds during the holi-
days," when the actual prediction was "four to seven
pounds."

CHAPTER 16

How to Lose Some Innards and Sound the Same: Internal Deletion Homophones

An internal deletion homophone is a word that becomes its own homophone when one of its internal letters is removed.

add	ad
aunt	ant
bee	be
bread	bred
callous	callus
cannon	canon
canvass	canvas
chord	cord
dessert	desert (*what is deserved*)
eave	eve

heard	herd
hoarse	horse
mooed	mood
scent	sent
two	to

INTERLUDE 3

A MUSICAL BREAK: WORDPLAY INVOLVING MISHEARD LYRICS, PUNS, AND PALINDROMES IN MUSIC

MUSICAL MONDEGREENS

JOHNNY RIVERS, "SECRET AGENT MAN"
Sounds like: Secret Asian man
Is really: Secret agent man

THE EAGLES, "HOTEL CALIFORNIA"
Sounds like: On a dark desert highway, cool whip in my hair
Is really: On a dark desert highway, cool wind in my hair

THE FOUR TOPS, "I CAN'T HELP MYSELF"
Sounds like: You left you picked your behind / And I kissed it a thousand times
Is really: You left your picture behind / And I kissed it a thousand times

SYBIL, "DON'T MAKE ME OVER"
Sounds like: Don't make me yodel
Is really: Don't make me over

ROLLING STONES, "BEAST OF BURDEN"
Sounds like: I'll never leave your pizza burning
Is really: I'll never be your beast of burden

LAURYN HILL, "KILLING ME SOFTLY"
Sounds like: Strummin' my brain with his fingers
Is really: Strummin' my pain with his fingers

DEEP PURPLE, "SMOKE ON THE WATER"
Sounds like: Slow-talking Walter, the fire-engine guy
Is really: Smoke on the water and fire in the sky

ALANIS MORRISETTE, "YOU OUGHTA KNOW"
Sounds like: The cross-eyed bear that you gave to me
Is really: Of the cross I bear that you gave to me

AEROSMITH, "DUDE (LOOKS LIKE A LADY)"
Sounds like: Do the Funky Lady
Is really: Dude looks like a lady

VAN MORRISON, "BROWN EYED GIRL"
Sounds like: Gunnin' down the old man / With a transistor radio
Is really: Goin' down the old mine / With a transistor radio

ALBERT HAMMOND, "IT NEVER RAINS IN SOUTHERN CALIFORNIA"
Sounds like: It never rains in California . . . Matadors
Is really: It never rains in California . . . Man, it pours

GRAND FUNK, "WE'RE AN AMERICAN BAND"
Sounds like: We're in America, man
Is really: We're an American band

ELTON JOHN, "TINY DANCER"
Sounds like: Hold me closer Tony Danza
Is really: Hold me closer tiny dancer

THE WEATHER GIRLS, "IT'S RAINING MEN"
Sounds like: Israeli men! Hallelujah!—Israeli men!
Is really: It's raining men! Hallelujah!—It's raining men!

KENNY ROGERS, "LUCILLE"
Sounds like: You picked a fine time to leave me, Lucille / With
   four hundred children and a crop in the field
Is really: You picked a fine time to leave me, Lucille / With
   four hungry children and a crop in the field

**VICKI LAWRENCE, "THE NIGHT THE LIGHTS WENT OUT IN
GEORGIA"**
Sounds like: The judge in the town's got love stains on his
   pants
Is really: The judge in the town's got bloodstains on his
   hands

LED ZEPPELIN, "WHOLE LOTTA LOVE"
Sounds like: I'm gonna give you every inch of my gloves
Is really: I'm gonna give you every inch of my love

**CROSBY, STILLS, NASH, AND YOUNG, "HELPLESSLY
HOPING"**
Sounds like: Helplessly hoping / Her hard-lickin' lover's
   nearby
Is really: Helplessly hoping / Her harlequin hovers nearby

QUEEN, "WE WILL ROCK YOU"
Sounds like: You've got mud on yo' face, front disc brakes
Is really: You've got mud on yo' face / You big disgrace

CRYSTAL GAYLE, "DON'T IT MAKE MY BROWN EYES BLUE"
Sounds like: Doughnuts make my brown eyes blue
Is really: Don't it make my brown eyes blue

ABBA, "LAY ALL YOUR LOVE ON ME"
Sounds like: I was in jail just before we met
Is really: I wasn't jealous before we met

EURYTHMICS, "SWEET DREAMS (ARE MADE OF THIS)"
Sounds like: Sweet dreams are made of cheese
Is really: Sweet dreams are made of this

SIMON AND GARFUNKEL, "THE SOUND OF SILENCE"
Sounds like: Silence like a casserole
Is really: Silence like a cancer grows

REM, "LOSING MY RELIGION"
Sounds like: Oh life is bigger / It's bigger than you / And you are knock-kneed
Is really: Oh life is bigger / It's bigger than you / And you are not me

THE MONKEES, "I'M A BELIEVER"
Sounds like: And then I saw her face / Now I'm gonna leave her
Is really: And then I saw her face / Now I'm a believer

NAZARETH, "LOVE HURTS"
Sounds like: Love Earth, love stars / Love Moon, and Mars
Is really: Love hurts, love scars / Love wounds, and mars

RAY PARKER JR., "GHOSTBUSTERS"
Sounds like: Who you gonna call? Gus Foster
Is really: Who you gonna call? GHOSTBUSTERS

MADONNA, "LA ISLA BONITA"
Sounds like: Last night I dreamt of some bagels
Is really: Last night I dreamt of San Pedro

COUNTRY SONG
TITLES WITH PUNS

"I Still Miss You, Baby, but My Aim's Gettin' Better"
"If You Can't Live without Me, Why Aren't You Dead Yet?"
"She Got the Gold Mine, I Got the Shaft"
"Because of the Cat-House, I'm in the Dog-House"
"How Can I Miss You If You Won't Go Away?"
"Please Bypass This Heart"
"The Pint of No Return"
"You Can't Have Your Kate and Edith, Too"
"Get Your Biscuits in the Oven and Your Buns in the Bed"
"Refried Dreams"

PALINDROMIC TITLES

Aoxomoxoa, Grateful Dead album
Olé ELO, Electric Light Orchestra (ELO) album
Satanoscillatemymetallicsonatas, Soundgarden album (also
    known as *SOMMS*)
SOS, ABBA single
UFO Tofu, Béla Fleck and The Flecktones album

CHAPTER 17

RT or DVS Words:
Grammagrams

Grammagrams are words such as *decay* that, when they are pronounced, consist entirely of letter sounds. Note that MC (master of ceremonies) and DJ (disc jockey) are formed from letters representing words and are not grammagrams but initialisms. The letters for grammagrams are popular on vanity license plates.

TWO-SYLLABLE GRAMMAGRAMS

any = NE
beady = BD
cagey = KG
cutie = QT
decay = DK
easy = EZ
empty = MT
envy = NV
essay = SA
excel = XL
excess = XS
icy = IC

ivy = IV
Kewpie = QP
seedy = CD
teepee = TP

THREE-SYLLABLE GRAMMAGRAMS

cesium = CZM
devious = DVS
effendi = FND (*Turkish title of respect*)
enemy = NME
envious = NVS
escapee = SKP
odious = ODS
opium = OPM
tedious = TDS

FOUR-SYLLABLE GRAMMAGRAMS

eminency = MNNC
anemone = NMNE
Arcadian = RKDN
excellency = XLNC

FIVE-SYLLABLE GRAMMAGRAMS

effeminacy = FMNSE
obediency = OBDNC
expediency = XPDNC

CHAPTER 18

How to Spell Chemical Elements Using Chemical Symbols: Chemograms

There are exactly twelve chemical elements whose names can be spelled using only elemental symbols from the periodic table.

Ar-Se-Ni-C = arsenic (*argon, selenium, nickel, carbon*)

As-Ta-Ti-Ne = astatine (*arsenic, tantalum, titanium, neon*)

Bi-Sm-U-Th = bismuth (*bismuth, samarium, uranium, thorium*)

C-Ar-B-O-N = carbon (*carbon, argon, boron, oxygen, nitrogen*)

Co-P-P-Er = copper (*cobalt, phosphorus, phosphorus, erbium*)

Ir-O-N = iron (*iridium, oxygen, nitrogen*)

Kr-Y-Pt-O-N = krypton (*krypton, yttrium, platinum, oxygen, nitrogen*)

P-H-Os-P-H-O-Ru-S = phosphorus (*phosphorus, hy-*

drogen, osmium, phosphorus, hydrogen, oxygen, ru-
thenium, sulfur)

Si-Li-Co-N = silicon (*silicon, lithium, cobalt, nitrogen*)

Ti-N = tin (*titanium, nitrogen*)

Xe-No-N = xenon (*xenon, nobelium, nitrogen*)

CHAPTER 19

Words That Can Strike a
Note: Piano Words

A piano word is a word each of whose letters can be played as a note on a musical instrument (such as *cabbage*). Large piano words are unusual because few large English words exist without using any letters from *H* through *Z*. There are very few unhyphenated piano words with eight letters; among the few are *debagged* and *cabbaged* (which can mean "stolen" or "filched").

PIANO WORDS CONTAINING FOUR OR MORE LETTERS

abed
accede
acceded
aced
adage
added
aged
babe
bade
baggage

bagged
bead
beaded
bedded
beef
cabbage
cabbaged
cadge
cadged
café
cage
caged
cede
dabbed
debagged
decade
deeded
deface
defaced
ebbed
edge
edged
efface
effaced
egad
egged
facade
faced
faded
feed
gabbed
gadded
gagged

CHAPTER 20

Every Letter Can Sometimes Refuse to Speak: Twenty-Six Silent Letters

One thing that makes English difficult to spell and pronounce is the silent letter. Much of English is derived from other languages, such as Greek, giving us such words as *ptomaine*, *psychology*, and *pterodactyl*. Although the French have given us great food and wine, they've also given us words such as *rendezvous*, which is not helpful to students who are told to spell words the way the sound. The following words contain silent letters:

A: bread, liar
B: debt, thumb
C: Connecticut, indict, science
D: handsome, Wednesday
E: height, tape, steak
F: halfpenny (*HAYP-nee or HAY-puh-nee*)
G: gnome, night, phlegm
H: bough, ghost, honor
I: business, thief, Sioux
J: rijsttafel (*RYST-tah-fel*)

EVERY LETTER CAN BE PRONOUNCED
IN A WORD WITHOUT APPEARING IN IT:
TWENTY-SIX SPOKEN BUT UNSEEN LETTERS

A: bouquet

B: Peiping (*BAY-ping*)

C: seal

D: Taoism (*DOW-izm*)

E: quay

F: cough

G: janitor

H: Navajo

I: gypsy

J: gesticulate

K: cay

L: W-shaped (*DUH-buhl yoo*)

M: grandpa (*GRAM-paw*)

N: comptroller

O: beau

P: hiccough

Q: cue

R: colonel

S: center

T: passed

U: ewe

V: of

W: once

X: necks

Y: wine

Z: xylem

K: blackguard (*BLAG-uhrd*)

L: Lincoln, talk

M: mnemonic

N: column, monsieur

O: country, people

P: cupboard, psychology, receipt, sapphire

Q: racquet

R: forecastle (*FOHK-suhl*)

S: aisle, debris, island, viscount

T: apostle, gourmet, listen

U: circuit, dough, gauge, plague

V: flivver, savvy (*The second V is silent: FLIV-uhr, SAV-ee.*)

W: answer, two, wrist

X: faux pas, grand prix, Sioux

Y: aye, crayon, prayer

Z: rendezvous

CHAPTER 21

Names That Fit Perfectly:
Euonyms

James R. Hoffa, the teamster leader who mysteriously disappeared had, as it turned out, an appropriate middle name: Riddle. Robert S. McNamara, U.S. secretary of defense from 1961 to 1968, struck people as strange when he was publicly opposed to Vietnam only after the war was over. In any event, he had a strange middle name: Strange. Actress Angelina Jolie is well named because her name literally means "pretty little angel." Chris Moneymaker, the actual name of the American poker player who won the main event of the 2003 World Series of Poker, is also well named because he turned $40 into $2.5 million.

Other famous people with apt names (or euonyms) are Sally Ride (the first American female astronaut in space), Larry Speakes (presidential press secretary under President Ronald Reagan), Gary Player (the famous golfer), and Tiger Woods (since wood is a golf club).

Here are some other euonyms:

Jeff Bagwell	MLB first baseman
Lloy [*sic*] Ball	American volleyball player
Layne Beachley	Australian world champion surfer
Chip Beck	professional golfer
Sara Blizzard	BBC weather presenter
Usain Bolt	Jamaican Olympic gold sprinter
Samantha Bond	actress in four James Bond movies
Marshall Brain	scientist and writer
Russell Brain	neurologist
Albert Champion	French road cycling champion
Reggie Corner	NFL cornerback
Margaret Court	tennis player
Thomas Crapper	manufacturer of Victorian toilets (*the slang use of the word* crap *predates him*)
Tim Duncan	NBA power forward and center
Rich Fairbank	founder and CEO of Capital One Financial Corporation
Cecil Grant Fielder	MLB power hitter
Jamie Gold	winner of 2006 World Series of Poker
Learned Hand	American judge
Vince Offer	infomercial host

Josh Outman	MLB pitcher
Larry Page	co-founder of Google
James Cash Penney	founder of JCPenney stores
Gary Player	professional golfer
Scott Player	NFL punter
Alto Reed	saxophonist
Marc Rich	billionaire financier
Bob Rock	rock music producer
John Wisdom	British philosopher

INTERLUDE 4

A NOMINAL BREAK: WORDPLAY INVOLVING THE OUTRAGEOUS NAMES OF REAL PEOPLE

Most of the following names come from *John Train's Most Remarkable Names*.

NAMES THAT BELONG OR HAVE BELONGED TO REAL PEOPLE

Tonsillitis Jackson: At a naval hospital in Balboa, California, attendants filled in a startling case history. The ailment was tonsillitis. The patient: Tonsillitis Jackson. Jackson was not the only family member with an inflamed name. Jackson, whose mother suffered from tonsillitis when he was born, had a brother and four sisters whose names were Meningitis, Appendicitis, Laryngitis, Peritonitis, and Jakeitis.

A. Toxen Worm: Worm, a well-known theatrical agent who was associated with Shubert theatrical enterprises, died in Paris of apoplexy. His passing was noted in the *New York Times*.

The Reverend Blanco White: The Reverend White was ordained a priest in 1800. His name was M. Blanco, but he adopted the name of White, English for "blanco." He was a professor of religion who renounced Christianity and abandoned the priesthood but later reembraced Christianity and was reordained.

Mrs. Belcher Wack Wack: When Mrs. Belcher Wack Wack was Miss Belcher, she married Mr. Wack and later married his brother.

Mr. Joynt: He was a marijuana analyst for the Royal Canadian Mounted Police in Alberta, Canada.

Dr. Richard (Dick) Chopp: Chopp is an Austin, Texas, urologist whose slogan is, I'm not kidding, "There are more vasectomies to be done."

Messrs. Bull and Schytt: The two were glaciologists in Geneva, Switzerland—no schytt.

Sir Cloudsley Shovel: He was a distinguished admiral in the British Royal Navy who at the end of his career ran the fleet on the rocks (Isles of Scilly) in 1707, drowning 2,000 men. He was killed by a peasant woman who coveted his emerald ring.

Dr. Alden G. Cockburn: He is a urologist working in New Mexico.

Mr. Cock Married Miss Prick: According to the *London Times*, the Pricks were united in 1963.

Mrs. Friendly Ley: A resident of Mission Hills, California, who had an accommodating name, Ley died unpleasantly as the revolver her husband was cleaning discharged.

Groaner Digger: According to *Today's Health*, Digger was an undertaker in Houston, Texas.

Fanny Fangboner: Fangboner was a nurse in Sandusky,

Ohio, possibly related to Humperdink Fangboner, a local lumber dealer.

Kim Yoo Suk: This South Korean pole vaulter competed at the 2004 Olympic Games.

Sue Yoo: Yoo, an American lawyer, married Matthew Murakami in December 2010.

I. C. Shivers: Shivers was an iceman.

John L. Senior, Junior: He was an aeronautical engineer who founded New York Airways, which provided helicopter service in the New York area until 1979.

Ima Hogg: Hogg, known as "the First Lady of Texas," was an American philanthropist, patron, and collector of the arts who came to be one of the most well-respected Texans during the twentieth century. Contrary to popular myth, Ima did not have a sister named Ura.

Halloween Burl Buggage: A resident of New Orleans, Louisiana, Buggage died in 2010.

Joy Bang: Bang, born in 1945, has been an actress and has appeared in several nonpornographic TV shows and movies, including Woody Allen's *Play It Again, Sam*, in which she played the date who was abducted by bikers.

Katz Meow: She was a resident of Hoquiam, Washington.

Lavender Sidebottom: Lavender Sidebottom was a masseuse at Elizabeth Arden's in New York City.

Mr. Clapp: He was a venereal disease counselor and lecturer for the county health service in San Mateo, California.

Larry Derryberry: Derryberry was the attorney general of Oklahoma from 1971 to 1979. There are less well-known men with the same name, including the Larry Derryberry of Molalla, Oregon, who had a thirty-year career with Sears and who died in 2010.

Any Day: Was included in the 1871 census for Crawshaw Booth, Lancashire, England.

Silence Bellows: Silence Bellows was an editor of the *Christian Science Monitor*.

Chief B. Crooke: Chief Crooke once headed the police force in Montgomery County, Maryland.

Major Minor: Major Minor was in the U.S. Army.

Mercy Bumpus: She was the wife of General Tom Thumb.

Mustafa Kunt: According to *John Train's Most Remarkable Names* and Larry Ashmead's *Bertha Venation*, Mustafa Kunt was the name of a Turkish military attaché. It is also the name of another Turk who was born in Ankara in 1978. The latter Mr. Kunt earned a master's degree at the Städel Art Academy and in 2008 had a solo exhibition titled "Vier Mustafa Kunt III" at the Museum Für Moderne Kunst in Frankfurt, Germany.

Newton Hooton: Hooton was a resident of Cambridge, Massachusetts.

Orange Marmalade Lemon: Lemon lived in Wichita, Kansas.

Void Null: Null, daughter of Thomas Jefferson Null, was a schoolteacher in San Diego, California.

Anil G. Shitole: Shitole lived in Rochester, New York.

Supply Clapp Thwing: Thwing graduated from Harvard in 1837.

Cumming & Gooing / Gooing & Cumming: In a 1959 central Los Angeles telephone directory, a firm of lawyers was listed under *C* as "Cumming & Gooing" and under *G* as "Gooing & Cumming." According to the September 19, 1959, *New Yorker* magazine, an observer couldn't tell whether the firm was "Cumming" or "Gooing."

Miss Pensive Cocke: Cocke, a woman with a semithoughtful name, was secretary of the U.S. Army Air Corps.

Private Parts: Private Parts was a soldier in the U.S. Army.

Dr. Zoltan Ovary: An immunologist (no, not a gynecologist) at New York University, Dr. Ovary conducted groundbreaking experiments that helped establish the mechanism setting off allergic reactions. He died in 2005 at age ninety-eight.

Amy Freeze: Freeze is the weekend meteorologist at WABC-TV in New York.

Hunter Fisher: Hunter Fisher started Anchorage's first taxidermy business.

Welcome Bender: Bender is a professor in Harvard's Department of Biological Chemistry and Molecular Pharmacology.

Yolanda Squatpump: Squatpump was a makeup artist on the set of the film *The Usual Suspects*.

CHAPTER 22

Welcome to the Department of Redundancy Department: Pleonasms

Nothing exceeds like excess. Pleonasm, from the Greek *plēon* (more) is the use of words unnecessary for clear expression. Some pleonastic phrases are idioms, such as *safe haven* and *tuna fish*. Other pleonastic phrases come from legalese, such as *null and void*, *each and all*, and *cease and desist*. Other pleonasms stem from ignorance of acronyms, such as *ABM missile* (antiballistic missile missile). Still other pleonasms are the result of ignorance of foreign terms, such as *a capella without musical instruments*.

COMMON PLEONASMS

a known carcinogen suspected of causing cancer
A.M. in the morning
ABS system (*antilock braking system system*)
absolutely essential
absolutely necessary
AC current (*alternating current current*)

ACT test (*American College Test test*)

advanced scouting

advanced warning

advance forward

affirmative yes

Amoco Oil Co.

and etc.

APL programming language (*a programming language programming language*)

ascend up

ATM machine (*automated teller machine machine*)

attach together

autobiography of my life

automatic ATM machine (*automatic automated teller machine machine*)

BASIC code (*Beginner's All-Purpose Symbolic Instruction Code code*)

basic fundamentals

beautiful vista to look upon

blood hemorrhage

boat marina

CAD design (*computer-aided design design*)

cash money

circulated around

classify into groups

climb up

close proximity

close scrutiny

CNN news network (*Cable News Network news network*)

coequal partners

cold ice

collaborate together

combined together

commuting back and forth

completely annihilated

completely empty

completely full

completely unanimous

component parts

connect up together

conniption fit

constant nagging

current incumbent

DC current (*direct current current*)

dead corpse

descend down

diametrically opposed

different variation

DMZ zone (*demilitarized zone zone*)

DOS operating system (*disk operating system operating system*)

downward descent

each and every

eliminate altogether

empty hole

empty space

end result

entirely eliminating

exact replica

exact same

existing condition

experiment someone was trying out

extra added features

favorable approval

fellow colleague

final end

final showdown

first conceived
forced compulsion
foreign imports
former graduate
former veteran
free gift
frozen tundra
general consensus of opinion
give and bequeath
GMT time (*Greenwich Mean Time time*)
good success
GOP party (*Grand Old Party party*)
grateful thanks
GRE exam (*Graduate Record Exam exam*)
have and hold
hear with one's own ears
HIV virus (*human immunodeficiency virus virus*)
hot water heater
HTML language (*hypertext markup language language*)
imminent at any moment
individual person
inquisitive busybody
invited guests
irregardless
ISBN number (*International Standard Book Number number*)
join together
joint cooperation
killed dead
knowledgeable expert
LAN network (*local area network network*)
LCD display (*liquid crystal display display*)
LED diode (*light emitting diode diode*)
lesbian woman

literate readers

live witness

living legend in his (or her) own time

long chronic illness

long litany

major breakthrough

malignant cancer

manually by hand

many frequent

mental thought

missing gaps

more unique

mutual cooperation

NATO organization (*North Atlantic Treaty Organization organization*)

near proximity

negative no

new discovery

new innovation

nostalgia for the past

not sufficient enough

old custom

oral conversation

original founder

original source

over again

overused cliché

pair of twins

past experience

past tradition

PC computer (*personal computer computer*)

persistent obsession

personal friend(ship)

PIN number (*personal identification number number*)

pizza pie
play actor
please RSVP (*please respond please*)
P.M. in the evening
polar opposites
positive yes
postponed until later
preplanning
present incumbent
pruned out
quite unique
rags and tatters
receded back
refer back
regular routine
repeat again
resulting effects
retreating back
revert back
round circle
round wheels
ruling junta
safe haven
safe sanctuary
SCSI Interface (*small computer system interface inter-
    face*)
seedling plant
see with one's own eyes
shape and form
sink down
small speck
specific examples
successful achievement
sudden impulse

sum total
surrounded on all sides
technical jargon
the hoi polloi (*the the many*)
tiny speck
top priority
true facts
tuna fish
12 o'clock midnight
12 o'clock noon
two-man tandem

ETYMOLOGICALLY REDUNDANT EXPRESSIONS

For those who like belaboring the obscure, consider the following etymologically redundant expressions:

rice paddy: Because *paddy* comes from a Malay word for "rice" (*padi*), the expression *rice paddy* is etymologically redundant.

cash box: Because *cash* (from Italian *cassa* or French *casse*) originally meant "money box," *cash box* is etymologically redundant.

hailstone: Because *hail* is derived from the Greek for "pebble" or "stone," *hailstone* is etymologically redundant.

head chef: Because *chef* comes from the French word for "head" (also used to mean "head cook"), *head chef* is etymologically redundant.

head of cabbage: Because *cabbage* means "head" (derived from the Latin *caput* via the Old French *caboche*), *head of cabbage* is etymologically redundant.

unexpected emergency
unexpected surprise
unhealthy sickness
university college student
unnecessary redundancies
unsolved mystery
UPC code (*universal product code code*)
useless and unnecessary
usual custom
vacillating back and forth
VIN number (*vehicle identification number number*)
wall mural
watching and observing
water hydrant
widow woman
widower man
with au jus
wordy and verbose
worldwide pandemic disease

CHAPTER 23

I'm Not Averse to Using a Verse: Charades

Charades are words that contain sets of words within them by respacing but not rearranging letters. The divisions between the shorter words need not match the division between the syllables. Indeed, charades can be interesting when the shorter words do not match syllables, as in *pigeon* (pig + eon), or in *outreached* (outré + ached). Charades appeared in English puzzles in the 1740s, though the name itself didn't appear until the 1770s.

abeam = a + beam; a + be + am
across = a + cross
adage = ad + age
alien = a + lien
alienation = a + lie + nation
alkaline = Al + Kaline (*baseball player*)
amiable = am + I + able
amok = am + ok
anatomy = an + a + to + my
artichoke = art + I + choke
atone = at + one

SEX-CHANGE CHARADES

A sex change charade is a two-word phrase or sentence made from a single word beginning with the prefix ex-. The letter s is added immediately before the ex- and to the ending of the original word, and then the word is separated into sex plus a second word.

exact = sex acts
exasperate = sex asperates
exchange = sex changes
exclaim = sex claims
excogitate = sex cogitates
excommunicate = sex communicates
expose = sex poses
expulse = sex pulses

atrophy = a + trophy
attendance = at + ten + dance
averse = a + verse
avoid = a + void
banana = ban + an + a
barflies = barf + lies
barmaid = barm + aid
barrage = bar + rage
beam = be + am
bean = be + an
beanstalk = beans + talk
beat = be + at
beauties = beau + ties
bewilder = be + wilder

brokerage = broke + rage
button = butt + on; but + ton
capacity = cap + a + city
caravan = car + a + van
Connecticut = connect + I + cut
daredevil = dared + evil
detergent = deter + gent
diplomatically = diplomatic + ally
discovery = disco + very
earshot = ears + hot
generation = gene + ration
handled = hand + led
heat = he + at
Hebrew = he + brew
history = hi + story
identity = id + entity; ID + entity
inaction = in + action
initiate = in + it + I + ate
irate = I + rate
Isabelle = is + a + belle
island = is + land
manslaughter = man's + laughter
martinis = Martin + is
mean = me + an
meant = me + ant
meat = me + at
mendacity = mend + a + city
mendicant = mend + I + can't; mend + I + cant
molestation = mole + station
molesting = mole + sting
mustache = must + ache
New Zealand = new + zeal + and
notable = no + table; not + able

CHARADES' LEAPFROGGING COUSINS: BOOKEND WORDS

A bookend word contains two shorter words, one formed by consecutive letters within the original word and the other formed by the remaining letters.

BEtrayER = beer + tray
DEbatER = deer + bat
DEmeanED = deed + mean
LIgameNT = lint + game
REsideNT = rent + side

novice = no + vice
nowhere = now + here
office = off + ice
oftentimes = of + ten + times
onus = on + us
overtax = overt + ax
passage = pass + age
penis = pen + is
pleasure = plea + sure
products = pro + ducts
psychotherapist = psycho + the + rapist
punished = pun + I + shed
rampant = ram + pant
reformatory = reform + a + Tory
reinforce = rein + force
signage = sign + age
significant = sign + if + I + can't
sunglasses = sung + lasses
theirs = the + IRS

therapist = the + rapist
together = to + get + her
tomorrow = tom + or + row
toreador = to + read + or
wasted = was + Ted
weeknight = wee + knight

CHAPTER 24

Making Every Other Letter Count: Alternades

An alternade is a word whose letters, taken alternatively, in strict sequence, make up at least two other words. Every letter must be used. The shorter words consist of either completely odd-numbered letters or completely even-numbered letters within the parent word. Depending on the length of the word, the component words can have unequal numbers of letters. For example, *board* makes *bad* (consisting of the first, third, and fifth letters of the parent word) and *or* (consisting of the second and fourth letters of the parent word). *Algeria* makes *Agra*, a city in India, and *lei*. An alternade is much rarer than a charade (daredevil = dared + evil), which isn't made up of alternating letters.

calliopes = clips + aloe
curtainless = cranes + utils
pained = pie + and
schooled = shoe + cold
spallation = Salto (*city in Uruguay*) + plain
triennially = tinily + renal
troupe = top + rue

truancies = Tunis (*city in Tunisa*) + race
waist = wit + as
waists = wit + ass

It is possible to have an alternade using every third letter, as in *lacerated* (let + are + cad).

CHAPTER 25

Words Carrying Synonymous Offspring: Kangaroo Words

Kangaroo words contain smaller words related in meaning to the larger, parent word. The smaller word is spelled with successive but not completely consecutive letters, such as *calumnies* contains *lies*, *destruction* contains *run*, and *instructor* contains *tutor*. Kangaroo words are so named because they, like kangaroo mothers, carry their little ones (joeys).

accustomed	used
acrid	acid
adroitness	art
affect	act
allocate	allot
amicable	amiable
apposite	apt
arena	area
asseverate	aver

balsam	balm
barren	bare
because	as
before	ere
blossom	bloom
brackets	braces
Brobdignagian	big
brush	bush
Budweiser	beer
burst	bust
capsule	case
catacomb	tomb
charge	care
chocolate	cocoa
christening	rite
closemouthed	mute
clue	cue
coldhearted	hard
compadres	cadre
complemented	complete
conjunction	union
container	can
contaminate	taint
contradictory	contrary
controlled	cool
cooled	cold
courtesy	curtsy

ROD L. EVANS

cozen	con
curtail	cut
damsel	dame
daub	dab
dazzle	daze
deceased	dead
deception	con
deliberated	debated
departed	dead
department	arm
depository	depot
desiderate	desire
destruction	ruin
deteriorate	rot
determine	deem
dice	die
disappointed	sad
discourteous	curt
displeasure	ire
disputation	spat
disseminated	sent
earlier	ere
egotist	egoist
encourage	urge
enjoyment	joy
entwined	tied
equilateral	equal

equitable	equal
evacuate	vacate
evidenced	evinced
exhausted	used
exhortation	oration
exists	is
expurgate	purge
fabrication	fiction
facade	face
fairly	fay
falsities	lies
feasted	ate *and* feted
felicitous	fit
forbiddance	ban
fountain	font
frangible	frail
fulminate	fume
healthier	haler
honorable	noble
hostelry	hotel
hurries	hies
illuminated	lit
imaginary	airy
impair	mar
impertinent	pert
incapability	inability
indolent	idle

inflammable	flammable
inheritor	heir
investigate	vet
irateness	ire
isolated	sole
joined	one
joviality	joy
knapsack	pack
latest	last
lighted	lit
lonely	only
market	mart
masculine	male
matches	mates
misinterpret	err
moisture	mist
municipality	city
myself	me
nourished	nursed
obligated	obliged
ornamented	ornate
outspoken	open
perambulate	amble
petrochemical	oil
pinioned	pinned
platter	plate
playfellow	pal

postured	posed
practicable	practical
practitioner	actor
prattle	prate
precipitation	rain
prematurely	early
proportionate	prorate
prosecute	sue
quiescent	quiet
rambunctious	raucous
rampage	rage
rapscallion	rascal
ravaging	raging
recline	lie
reduplicate	replicate
regulate	rule
rendition	edition
respite	rest
restrain	rein
retrogress	regress
revived	revved
revolution	revolt
rotund	round
routine	rut
salvage	save
satiate	sate
satisfied	sated

scion	son
sculpt	cut
separate	part
shadowy	shady
slithered	slid
sparse	spare
splatter	spatter
splinter	split
splotch	spot
steamy	seamy
stocking	sock
stricken	sick
strives	tries

ANTI-KANGAROO WORDS

Anti-kangaroo words, by the way, contain their antonyms, such as *covert*, which contains *overt*.

animosity	amity
communicative	mute
courteous	curt
effective	effete
exacerbate	abate
fabricate	fact
feast	fast
friend	fiend
pest	pet
prurient	pure

struggled	tugged
substandard	bad
supervisor	superior
supremacist	racist
tolerate	let
tosspot	sot
transgression	sin
twitch	tic
unanimity	unity
unsightly	ugly
variegated	varied
welded	wed
wriggle	wiggle
yearning	yen

CHAPTER 26

Words That Are So Nice They Got Named Twice: Tautonyms

A tautonym is a word or name consisting of two identical parts, one following the other, such as *murmur*. Most tautonyms, as the Father of Logology Dmitri Borgmann once observed, are un-English in etymology, meaning, and appearance. The tautonyms most familiar to us are usually hyphenated and consist of recognizable English, such as *fifty-fifty*, *twenty-twenty*, *pretty-pretty*, and *goody-goody*.

Tautonyms have been used in biological nomenclature to describe a genus and a species. Many people are familiar with *Bison bison* (American bison), though fewer may know *Gorilla gorilla* (western gorilla) and still fewer may know *Mephitis mephitis* (striped skunk), *Mops mops* (Malayan free-tailed bat), and *Troglodytes troglodytes* (Eurasian wren).

Tautonyms are prohibited in botanical nomenclature, though occasionally a redundant description can appear incognito, such as *Arctostaphylos uva-ursi*, which means "bearberry" twice, in Greek and Latin, respectively, as in the English words *arctoid* and *ursine*.

benben
beriberi
brubru
choo-choo
couscous
froufrou
furfur
grugru
guitguit
hotshots
ipilipil
kavakava
kumkum
murmur
muumuu
nagnag
paepae
pawpaw
pitpit
piupiu
pom-pom
sapsap
Sarsar
semsem
so-so
tartar
testes
titi
toatoa
tom-tom

tsetse
ulaula
verver
wou-wou
zoozoo

CHAPTER 27

Words That Carry Twins:
Internal Tautonyms

A tautonym, as noted in the last chapter, is a word consisting of two or more identical parts, such as *testes*. An internal tautonym is a word that has a tautonym within it, such as *nonsense*.

alfalfa
assassin
assessed
barbarous
Chihuahua
Cincinnati
contented
fibrobronchitis
fiddledeedee
furfuraceous
instantaneous
kinkiness
Mississippi
metastasis
nannander
nonsense
obsesses

possessed
quaquaversal
redeeded
redredge
satiation
seismism
sentential
Shoshone
singing
stomachache
superperfect
tinting
versers

CHAPTER 28

Lox Is Smoked Salmon or Liquid Oxygen: Portmanteau Words

Portmanteau words are words formed by combining two other words, such as in *smog* (smoke + fog) and *brunch* (breakfast + lunch). The term comes from French *porter* (to carry) and *manteau* (cloak) and can describe a large suitcase consisting of two parts that fold together. A portmanteau word carries another word.

affluenza = affluence + influenza (*extreme materialism reflected in overworking and excessive debt*)

anacronym = anachronistic + acronym (*a word that began as an acronym but is no longer known as an acronym, such as* laser, *which originally stood for light amplification by stimulated emission of radiation*)

anticipointment = anticipation + disappointment (*the feeling one gets when a product doesn't live up to its hype; in computer slang, it describes anticipating a*

good, affordable product that one knows will immi-
nently be obsolete)

bacne = back + acne (*zits on one's back*)

bromance = bro + romance (*a close but nonsexual rela-
tionship between men; coined by editor Dave Carnie
in the skateboard magazine* Big Brother)

cellopane = cell + pain (*an annoyingly loud cell phone
user*)

chatterati = chatter + -ati (*talking heads, pundits, col-
umnists, and talk show hosts collectively*)

craptacular = spectacular + crappy (*spectacularly crappy*)

cryptonoia = crypto- + -noia (*the paranoid tendency to
read negative meaning into things unjustifiably*)

dorkumentary = dork + documentary (*a documentary
on dorky subjects such as sci-fi, computers, or technology*)

doughmance = dough + romance (*dating someone just
for expensive gifts and lavish dates*)

fauxpology = faux + apology (*an apology that expresses
no responsibility for the undesirable outcome*)

flatuloquist = flatulence + ventriloquist (*a person who
has the ability to throw his or her fart, much as a
ventriloquist can throw his or her voice*)

fram = friend + spam (*unsolicited, impersonal e-mail
from a friend*)

frankenfood = Frankenstein + food (*genetically altered
food*)

frenemy = friend + enemy (*someone who pretends to be
a friend but is really an enemy*)

jumbrella = jumbo + umbrella (*large umbrella over an
outside table at a café or coffee house*)

lolmate = LOL + soulmate (*a person with whom one
shares funny e-mails*)

manorexic = man + anorexic (*a man who wants to be skinny and lack muscle tone*)

manscaping = man + landscaping (*removing unwanted body hair from a man*)

neologasm = neologism + orgasm (*the intensely pleasurable sensation generated by using, hearing, or coining a new word or phrase*)

ninjury = ninja + injury (*an injury of unknown or mysterious origin*)

podience = podcast + audience (*the people who listen to a podcast or, generally, people who listen to podcasts*)

Portlorgasm = Portland + orgasm (*a news feature viewed by the speaker or the writer as fawning over Portland, Oregon, such as its approach to transportation, food cart scene, or housing*)

procrasturbate = procrastinate + masturbate (*to waste time by masturbating*)

prostitot = prostitute + tot (*a young girl whose makeup and style of dress make her look like a prostitute*)

sexiled = sex + exiled (*to be unable to go into one's

room, *dorm, or apartment because one's roommate needs privacy for sex*)

southmaw = southpaw + maw (*one who eats primarily with the left side of one's mouth*)

stalkumentary = stalk + documentary (*a documentary produced by stalking a person*)

CHAPTER 29

Punishment: Fun with Puns

The pun is a form of wordplay suggesting at least two meanings by exploiting the multiple meanings of the same word or of similar-sounding words. Not all puns are created equal. Some require little or no sophistication; others, including those from Shakespeare, Oscar Wilde, and George Carlin, sometimes require large vocabularies or a good deal of linguistic sophistication.

Some of the best puns have circulated across the Internet without attribution, meaning that we can't be sure who originated them.

The butcher backed up into the meat grinder and got a little behind in his work.

Did you hear about the guy whose left side was cut off? He's all right now.

If you don't pay your exorcist, you get repossessed.

The thief who stole a calendar got twelve months.

A bicycle can't stand alone; it is two tired.

A backward poet writes inverse.

Police were called to a daycare where a three-year-old was resisting a rest.

I wondered why the baseball was getting bigger. Then it hit me.

To write with a broken pencil is pointless.

A chicken crossing the road: poultry in motion.

A boiled egg is hard to beat.

The guy who fell into an upholstery machine was fully recovered.

Show me a piano falling down a mineshaft, and I'll show you A-flat miner.

INTERLUDE 5

A COMMERCIAL BREAK: WORDPLAY INVOLVING PUNS AND FUNNY HOMOPHONES USED IN BUSINESSES

BUSINESS SIGNS WITH WORDPLAY

This section consists of funny business signs and slogans that are funny precisely because of puns, malapropisms, or double entendres (ambiguity that often involves a risqué interpretation). Most of the examples are intentionally funny, but some are ironic or funny because of ambiguity unintended by their authors. When an electrician has a truck carrying the words "We'll remove your shorts," we have an intentional pun. When a maternity shop has a sign saying "Closed on Labor Day," there is probably no pun intended, though some of us will laugh anyway.

Slogan for a septic tank cleaning business: We're #1 in the #2 business.

On a septic tank truck: Your poo is our pleasure.

On a septic tank truck: Yesterday's meals on wheels.

On a plumbing and septic tank truck: If it don't [*sic*] go down, call Brown.

On a plumber's truck: We repair what your husband fixed.

At a Maine restaurant: Open 7 days a week and weekends.

At Dirty Dicks Crab House in Virginia Beach, Virginia: I got my crabs from Dirty Dicks.

At a Massachusetts birdwatching area: Parking for birds only.

At a New York drugstore: We dispense with accuracy.

At a New York medical building: Mental Health Prevention Center.

At a New York restaurant: Customers who find our waitresses rude ought to see the manager.

Slogan for a mattress company: Come to us for the best lay in town.

Slogan of Cromer's (a seller of peanuts, popcorn, candy, and concession equipment): Guaranteed Worst in Town.

At a business in Norfolk, Virginia: Sorry, we're open.

At a transmission repair business in Columbus, Ohio: Get your shift together at Metro Transmission.

At a gynecologist's office: Dr. Jones, at your cervix.

At a proctologist's office: To expedite your visit, please back in.

Slogan of Wenneman Meat Co. in St. Libory, Illinois: You can't beat our meat!

At a radiator repair shop: Best place in town to take a leak.

At a plastic surgeon's office: Hello. May we pick your nose?

In a self-serve laundry: Automatic washing machines. Please remove all your clothes when the light goes out.

In a gym: Merry Fitness and a Happy New Rear!

In a department store: Bargain Basement Upstairs.

Slogan of Duct Doctor, a Canadian business: Sucking Professionally.

At a dental office: Be true to your teeth, or they will be false to you.

At a disco: Smarts is the most exclusive disco in town. Everyone welcome.

At a towing service: We don't charge an arm and a leg. We want tows.

At a tire shop in Milwaukee, Wisconsin: Invite us to your next blowout.

At a pizza shop: 7 days without pizza makes one weak.

FUNNY NAMES OF REAL BUSINESSES

Bead It = bead store in Santa Cruz, California

Beauty and the Bistro = restaurants in the United States

Booked Solid = used bookstore in Bradford, Vermont

Bullshifter's = manual transmission/clutch repair shop in San Jose, California

Citizen Canine = dog kennel in Oakland, California

Curl Up & Dye = beauty salons in the United States

Cyclepath = bicycle store in Hayward and San Mateo, California

Dewey, Cheatam, and Howe = restaurant in Spokane, Washington

Doggie Style = dog grooming business in North Highlands, California

Effin Computers = on-site computer repair in Westport, Connecticut

Escape From New York Pizza = restaurants in San Francisco, California

Garden of Eat'n = restaurant in Utopia, Texas

Hannah & Her Scissors = beauty salon in Miami Beach, Florida

It's a Crewel World = stitchery shops in the United States

Linoleum Dicks = floor covering store, San Jose, California

Many Happy Returns = tax preparation business in St. Petersburg, Florida

Murphy's Paw = doggie gift store in Pleasanton, California

Pizza My Heart = restaurants in San Francisco, California

Salt and Battery = fish and chips restaurants in Brisbane, Australia

Salvador Molly's Restaurant = restaurant in Portland, Oregon

The Best Little Hairhouse In Town = beauty salon in Camp Springs, Maryland

The Grill from Ipanema = Brazilian restaurant in Washington, DC

Wok N Roll = restaurants in the United States

FUNNY NAMES OF REAL LAW FIRMS

Boring & Leach in Guymon, Oklahoma

Bickers & Bickers in Murrysville, Pennsylvania (*a husband-and-wife team*)

Cummings & Lockwood in Connecticut and Florida

Harness, Dickey, & Pierce in Michigan, Missouri, Virginia, and Oregon

Lawless & Lawless in San Francisco, California

Lawless & Lynch in Jamaica, New York

Low, Ball, & Lynch in San Francisco, California

Alicia A. Slaughter in Los Angeles, California (*a personal injury specialist*)

Allen, Allen, Allen & Allen in Richmond, Virginia (*if Allen can't help you, try Allen, or Allen, or Allen*)

Payne & Fears in California and Nevada

CHAPTER 30

Phony Opposites: Phantonyms

A phantonym is a word or phrase that appears to be opposite in meaning to another word or phrase but isn't. For example, something inflammable can be inflamed as quickly as something flammable. We have *flammable* because many people think that the *in-* in *inflammable* means "not," as in *inattentive*. The *in-* is actually part of *inflame*, so that *inflammable*, when used literally, means "capable of being readily inflamed."

ahead	afoot
back up	back down
badly	goodly
breakdown	break up
canner	canter
canny	uncanny
cargo	bus stop
catalog	dogwood

catwalk	dogtrot
coffee	coffer
downfall	uprise
downright	upright
enrage	outrage
extinct	instinct
famous	infamous
forgive	forget
founder	loser
fraction	infraction
giveaway	getaway
give in	take out
give up *or* put up	take down
hardly	softly
headlights	footlights
hereafter	therefore
hotheads	cold feet
inception	exception
incite	excite
increment	excrement
in-laws	outlaws
inning	outing
input	outtake
intend	extend
layoff	standoff
layout	stand-in
left off	Right on!

Lord Haw-Haw (*propagandist*)	Lady Gaga
lowlands	high seas
maternity dress	paternity suit
mistaking	misgiving
nighthawk	mourning dove
offset	onset
outcome	income
outgrown	ingrown
outhouse	in-house
outlay	inlay
outtake	intake
overlay	understand
pair	impair
pale	impale
pertinent	impertinent
put off	take on
put-on	put-off
put-up	put-down
rundown	run-up
shut-out	shut-in
startle	stopple
sit-in	standout
takeoff	take on
turndown	turn up
undergo	overcome
understand	underlie

undertow	overhaul
upright	downright
walk-on	run off
walk-up	run down
walkout	run in

VICTOR VICTORIA: RELATED OR SYNONYMOUS PHANTONYMS

Some phantonyms are about as different as flapjacks and pancakes. That is to say, they describe the same thing. Others describe clearly related but sometimes distinguishable things, such as *valuable* and *invaluable* (as in a *valuable car*, which may be expected to have high market value, and an *invaluable experience*, which needn't have any market value).

CRAZY ENGLISH

Because it was cold as hell and we were anxious, we had trouble deciding whether to slow down or to slow up, and then we decided to stand down before eating vegetarian meatballs. Charlie's body was malfunctioning: his nose ran while his feet smelled. John thought he'd won the lottery but was informed that he had less than a slim chance; he had a fat chance. One man's house burned up as another man's burned down, requiring both to get in touch with insurance agents who asked them to fill out forms by filling them in. The first man lost quite a few valuable items, whereas the second man lost quite a lot.

---

barred	debarred
bone	debone
burn up	burn down
drop everything	hold everything
fat chance	slim chance
fill in	fill out
heritable	inheritable
loose	unloose
quite a few	quite a lot
ravel	unravel
restive	restless
shameful	shameless
slow up	slow down
unremorseless	remorseless
valuable	invaluable

CHAPTER 31

Every Picture Tells a Word: Rebuses

A rebus is a word picture in which letters and words are manipulated for their visual features. The meaning of the word *rebus* (Latin for "by things") is easily seen in the Latin phrase, *non verbis sed rebus* (not by words but by things). Accordingly, a rebus is a representation of a word or phrase by pictures, symbols, or letters unusually displayed. In the Middle Ages, the rebus was a popular heraldic expression to denote surnames, as when the name *Salmon* was represented by three salmon fish. Modern rebuses often occur in wordplay. Take a look at the following:

eggs

―――

light

represents "eggs over light." And *sbduoel* can be read as "mixed doubles." Here are some more:

Gegs = scrambled eggs

$$\frac{man}{board} = \text{man overboard}$$

$$\frac{under}{man} = \text{man down under or man under}$$

$$\frac{mind}{matter} = \text{mind over matter}$$

lev el = split level

death/life = life after death

ecnalg = glance backward

drnkis = mixed drinks

FECpoxTION = smallpox infection

esroh = horseback

IKD = mixed-up kid

T
O
U   = touchdown
C
H

iii

—— = circles under the eyes

ooo

taoc = turncoat

sammoc = inverted commas

98.6 MDJD = 98.6 degrees

ARupMS = up in arms

you just me = just between you and me

stool he fell stool = he fell between two stools

CHAPTER 32

How to Lose Your Head and Still Live (Sort Of): Beheadments

Although people don't function without their heads, words are more adaptive: A word can lose its first letter and become another word. The largest common beheadable words are *emotionlessness* (motionlessness), *gastronomically* (astronomically), and *treasonableness* (reasonableness).

beagle	eagle
bone	one
bonus	onus
breach	reach
bread	read
cache	ache
cash	ash
chose	hose
cinch	inch
climb	limb

close	lose
clover	lover
coverage	overage
cram	ram
crank	rank
devil	evil
drink	rink
fowl	owl
fox	ox
gamble	amble
glove	love
grumble	rumble
hover	over
lawful	awful
ledge	edge
orange	range
paged	aged
pirate	irate
stinker	tinker
stow	tow
swanker	wanker
swear	wear
tears	ears
there	here
trim	rim
trope	rope
vague	ague

wasp	asp
where	here
whose	hose
women	omen
yours	ours

CHAPTER 33

How to Lose Your Tail and Gain a New Identity: Curtailments

Just as a word can sometimes lose its first letter and still partially survive (usually as an unrelated word), so a word can sometimes lose its last letter and still survive (again, usually as an unrelated word). Accordingly, *brass* can become *bras* and *bugless* can become *bugles*.

apex	ape
area	are
badger	badge
bare	bar
beard	bear
beer	bee
board	boar
boast	boas

brassiere	brassier
camel	came
care	car
clothe	cloth
daisy	dais
deadliness	deadlines
discuss	discus
diverse	divers
earl	ear
first	firs
handless	handles
hate	hat
heath	heat
heaven	heave
hero	her
honest	hones
honey	hone
is	I
lather	lathe
leaven	leave
pearl	pear
priest	pries
quartz	quart
rabbit	rabbi
ration	ratio
saltiness	saltines

ROD L. EVANS

shrivel	shrive
spar	spa
suite	suit
vial	via
weary	wear

CHAPTER 34

Two-Faced Words: Contronyms

Sometimes words have two or more (even many more) meanings. Occasionally words can have *opposite* meanings, a recipe for confusion. Although words with many meanings are common, words with contrary or opposite meanings are unusual. Sometimes their contrary meanings still exist because of old idiomatic expressions, such as *cleave unto one's husband*, in which *cleave* can mean "to cling to" rather than "to split." In any event, the context will usually clarify which of the contrasting meanings is intended. Sometimes contronyms are known as Janus-faced words, after the Roman god of beginnings and transitions, most often depicted as having two faces, turned in opposite directions.

aloha

hello: Aloha! I'm glad that I have arrived.
good-bye: I'm glad to be going home. Aloha!

anabasis

military advance: Napoleon's anabasis into Russia was a serious mistake.
military retreat: Sometimes a military leader will conduct an anabasis to live to fight another day.

apology

admission of fault: Because Charlie didn't appear to be remorseful, we didn't accept his apology.
defense of one's words or action: During his trial Socrates gave an apology, defending not only his actions but also his way of life.

aught

all: For aught we know, the next Republican nominee for the presidency may be someone hardly known before the nomination.
nothing: The author worked hard but never got the manuscript accepted and so received aught for it.

below par

below average: Her performance on the Miller Analogies Test was below par for her major.
above average—that is, a score of fewer strokes than usual for a particular hole in golf: The excellent golfer was used to shooting below par.

bimonthly

every two months: This year's second bimonthly meeting was in April.

twice a month (semimonthly): February's bimonthly meetings will be on the first and the fourteenth.

bolt

to secure: I bolted the door before I went to sleep.
to depart: The boy bolted out of the room.

bound

restrained: We were bound by rules.
to spring: Conrad came bounding into the room to get some pizza.

buckle

to fasten: Please buckle your belt.
to come undone: We must be relentless and not buckle under pressure.

cheerio

hello: Cheerio! I'm delighted to have arrived in London.
good-bye: I've enjoyed my visit here and want to thank you for your hospitality. Cheerio!

cleave

to separate: We used the ax to cleave the log.
to adhere firmly: The preacher exhorted the man and his wife to cleave unto each other.

clip

to attach: Clip the note to the paper.
to remove: Please clip his hair.

commencement

beginning: This, our first meeting, is the commencement of an important organization.
conclusion: The commencement exercises marked the end of the graduation.

custom

something that is a long-established practice by many people: It was a custom to remove one's shoes when entering homes.
a modifier to indicate something that has been specially created to suit individual taste: The suit I bought was custom-made.

deceptively smart

smarter than one appears: Although President Truman didn't have much formal education and would sometimes wear unfashionable clothes, he was deceptively smart.
dumber than one appears: In the film *Being There*, Chance the Gardener (a.k.a. Chauncey Gardiner), played brilliantly by Peter Sellers, was a deceptively smart person who emitted TV-informed utterances mistaken for profundity.

discursive

proceeding coherently from topic to topic: The writer was trained as a logician so that his writings reflected discursive reasoning rather than intuitive insight.

moving aimlessly from topic to topic: Trying to see a logical vein of reasoning in Charlie Sheen's manic, discursive outbursts is like trying to nail Jell-O to a wall.

downhill

progressively easier (when describing a difficulty): Now that we have public support and ample funds, implementing our projects is all downhill from here.

progressively worse (when describing a status or condition): Unfortunately, her health went downhill.

dress

to put items on: I needed to dress before leaving for work.

to remove items from: The cook needed to dress the chicken for cooking.

dust

to remove material: We decided to dust the furniture.

to lay down material: The pilot was paid to dust the crops.

enjoin

to prohibit: The court order enjoined Ron from visiting his former wife.

to prescribe: Prince Hamlet was enjoined by the ghost of his father to revenge his father's murder.

fast

moving rapidly: The car was moving fast down the highway.
firmly in one place: The glue held the sign fast.

first degree

most severe (as in murder): The state decided to charge the man with first-degree murder.
least severe (as in burns): John was thankful that his burns were only first degree.

fix

to restore or repair: We thanked him for fixing our dock.
to castrate: At six months old, the cat was fixed.

flog

to criticize harshly: If the federal government had shut down over budgetary disagreements, many people would have flogged both major political parties.
to promote aggressively: Much money was spent to flog the new product so that people would know about it.

garnish

to enhance or decorate (as food): The cook garnished my entrée with Chinese vegetable leaves.

to take a part of someone's earnings in discharge of a debt: The court demanded that the man's earnings be garnished to pay for overdue child support.

give out

to produce: We gave out our best effort.
to stop producing: Their energy gave out.

go off

to begin: My alarm clock began to go off at seven o'clock in the morning.
to end: My lights must go off at nine at night.

grade

incline: Hiking became more difficult as we walked up the steep grade of the mountain path.
ground level: The underpinning of the tower was above grade.

handicap

advantage: The weakest golfer was given a handicap because he needed the extra shots to compete against the strongest players.
disadvantage: His lack of experience was a handicap.

help

to assist: If you need me to help you on your homework, please call me.

to prevent: Mary was criticized for something she couldn't help.

hold up

to support: Thanks for holding up your end.
to hinder: His intervention is beginning to hold up our progress.

impregnable

invulnerable: Because of his location in rough terrain and his powerful army, the dictator was impregnable to the rebels.
able to be impregnated: Because the young woman was impregnable, she always used birth control.

left

departed from: John left the school after his last class that day.
remained: After Sarah bought her land, she had no money left.

liege

a sovereign lord: The liege was owed allegiance and service from his subjects.
a loyal subject: The liege was protected by his feudal lord, who allowed the liege to work the land.

mean

average: A man of mean intelligence will probably find it difficult to teach advanced physics.

excellent: Joe Edley, the only person to have won America's National Scrabble Championship three times, plays a mean game.

moot

debatable: Jean's controversial remarks were moot.
no longer debatable: Because the authorities have made an irrevocable decision, the issue is now moot.

mortar

material for sticking things together: Bricks require mortar to stick together.
device for blowing things apart: A mortar shell blew apart the brick wall.

out

invisible: Please turn the lights out.
visible: The stars came out.

out of

outside: The baby fell out of the crib.
inside: Janet works out of her home.

overlook

to look over: The supervisor was paid to overlook the work to prevent problems.
to fail to look over: They miscalculated because they overlooked some expenses.

put out

to generate: You put out a great effort.
to extinguish: The firefighters put out the fire.

qualified

competent: We believed that the first candidate should get the job because she was the most highly qualified.
limited: The garage sale was a qualified success.

quiddity

a trifling point: The man's trivial objections were quiddities, distracting us from the central issue.
the essential nature of a thing: Socrates wanted to know the quiddity of piety and other ethical concepts.

quite

completely: Roger wasn't quite mistaken because part of what he was asserting was true.
to a great extent: The man is quite tall but hardly a giant.

ravel

to entangle: After Sarah pulled apart the fabric, the threads got raveled, falling into a tangled mess.
to disentangle: You'll need to ravel out the intricacies of your plan.

rent

to buy use of: After selling their home, the family looked for an apartment to rent.

to sell use of: Will you rent me a room?

root

to implant firmly: It is important for parents to root useful values into their children.

to remove completely: We must root out those students who really don't want to be in our organization.

sanction

approval: If a boxing match doesn't receive the sanction of the governing authorities, its results won't upset officially recognized standings.

coercive measure to discourage or punish behavior: Several nations adopted sanctions against the rogue nation for violations of international law.

scan

to inspect thoroughly: We didn't have time to scan the contract.

to glance casually: Please take time to scan the roll for your name.

screen

to view: The inspector began to screen the suitcases.

to conceal: The smuggler tried to screen the contraband to prevent being caught by the customs agent.

seed

to plant seeds in (land, for example): We need to seed the land now if we are to have crops during harvest-time.

to remove the seeds from (fruit): The watermelon has been seeded.

shank

the latter or remaining part, especially of a period of time: The class held at nine at night was at the shank of the school day.

the early or primary part of a period of time: It's only 6:30 at night, the shank of the evening.

skinned

covered with or as if with skin: The fuselage and wings were skinned with steel or titanium alloys.

stripped of the skin, peel, rind, or other outer covering: The fish was skinned and dressed.

stain

to color: We wanted to stain the desk to make it look more attractive.

to discolor: If you spill grape juice on the cloth, you'll stain it.

strike

to hit: Some people strike while the iron is hot; others strike until the iron is hot.

to miss (in baseball): The baseball player hated to strike out.

table

to propose (in the United Kingdom): Parliamentary representatives tabled some popular bills to please their constituents.

to set aside (in the United States): Members of the relevant congressional committee decided to table the bill until it could receive more support.

temper

to moderate or soften: We need to temper our anger with compassion.

to toughen: The manufacturer tempered the steel with additives to make it stronger.

trim

to add to (as in decorating): The kids loved to trim the Christmas tree.

to cut away: Please ask someone to trim your hair.

unbending

inflexible: Her commitment to improving her level of fitness was unbending.

given to relaxation: Drinks were served at the unbending party.

variety

one type (as of a fruit): Sheree's favorite variety of apple was Winesap.

many types: It is important to eat a variety of food.

weather

to hold up or bear: The ship weathered the storm.

to wear away: The tides increasingly weathered the rocks.

wind up

to end: It was time to wind up the meeting.

to start up (a watch): If I'm going to use that watch, I'll need to wind it up.

with

alongside: France fought with America against England.

against: Joe would sometimes fight with his wife.

to prohibit: The law enjoined the man from making contact with the woman he had stalked.

CHAPTER 35

There's a Sewer in the Sewer: Heteronyms

Heteronyms are words with identical spellings but different meanings and pronunciations. In short, they are homographs but not homophones (such as *no* and *know*). Because heteronyms are pronounced differently from words spelled the same, they are less likely to confuse listeners than readers. (By the way, words that have identical spellings and pronunciations but different meanings are homonyms, such as *left* (past tense of *leave*) and *left* (opposite of the direction right).

bass = an edible spiny-finned freshwater and marine fish *and* a large musical drum having a cylindrical body with two heads: A bass was painted on the bass drum.

close = near *and* to shut: When you're close to the door, please close it.

console= the desk from which an organ is played *and* to alleviate grief: When the organist found termites in the console, I tried to console her.

desert = to turn away from a previous commitment *and* a region with almost no rainfall: The soldier tried to desert in the desert.

does = present third-person singular of *do and* adult female deer: The buck does funny things around does.

dove = any of various smaller wild pigeons *and* to descend precipitously: The dove dove on high.

lead = to guide on a way *and* a soft, heavy gray metal: Jeff could lead if he could get the lead out.

minute = sixty seconds *and* tiny: I had only a minute to go into minute detail.

number = an arithmetical total *and* becoming desensitized: After she received a number of injections, her gums grew number.

object = to take exception to *and* a visible or tangible thing: Please don't object to the object.

present = to furnish to provide (as a person) with something *and* a gift: I want to present the present.

produce = to make or grow something *and* fruit, vegetables, and other things that farmers grow: The farm used to produce produce.

putting = hitting a golf ball with a light stroke *and* placing on one's body: It is difficult to break one's leg putting on a golf course or putting on one's shoes.

refuse = to reject *and* waste or rubbish: The dump was so full that it had to refuse our refuse.

resigned = accepted as inevitable *and* signed (one's name) again: She was resigned to the fact that the contract would have to be resigned.

sake = end or purpose *and* a Japanese alcoholic beverage made from rice: When we asked why he stole the alcohol, he said he did it for the sake of sake.

sow = adult female pig *and* to plant or scatter seed: We wanted to know how the farmer taught his sow to sow.

tear = to make a rent in *and* a drop of clear saline fluid

secreted by the lacrimal gland: When Donna saw a tear in her dress, she shed a tear.

wind = a natural movement of air at any speed *and* to move so as to encircle: The wind was so strong that we couldn't wind the sail.

wound = to encircle or cover with something pliable *and* a bodily injury: The bandage was wound around the wound.

INTERLUDE 6

A LITERARY BREAK: WORDPLAY INVOLVING AUTHORS' NAMES AND BOOK TITLES

AUTHORS WHOSE HOMOPHONIC NAMES SOUND CURIOUSLY RELATED TO THEIR SUBJECTS

Jane Arbor wrote *The Cypress Garden* (Winnipeg, Canada: Harlequin Books, 1969).

Claude Balls wrote *Shy Men, Sex, and Castrating Women* (Trexlertown, PA: Polemic Press, 1985).

William Battie wrote *A Treatise on Madness* (London: J. Whiston and B. White, 1758).

Cyril Berry wrote *Winemaking with Canned and Dried Fruit* (Andover, UK: Amateur Winemaker, 1968).

Clara Louise Burnham wrote *The Inner Flame: A Novel* (Boston: Houghton Mifflin, 1912).

Geoff Carless wrote *Motorcycling for Beginners* (East Ardsley, UK: EP Publishing, 1980).

J. N. Chance wrote *The Abel Coincidence* (London: Robert Hale, 1969).

W. Chappell wrote *The Preacher; or, The Art and Method of Preaching* (London: Edward Farnham, 1656).

William A. Christian wrote *Oppositions of Religious Doctrines* (London: Macmillan, 1972).

Edward H. Clinkscale wrote *A Musical Offering* (New York: Pendragon Press, 1977).

Douglas J. Cock wrote *Every Other Inch a Methodist* (London: Epworth Press, 1988).

Elizabeth Dyer wrote *Textile Fabrics* (Boston: Houghton Mifflin, 1923).

Harry Belleville Eisberg wrote *Fundamentals of Arctic and Cold Weather Medicine and Dentistry* (Washington, DC: Research Division, Bureau of Medicine and Surgery, 1949).

Frank Finn wrote *The Boy's Own Aquarium* (London: Country Life and George Newnes, 1922).

Paul J. Gillete wrote *Vasectomy: The Male Sterilization* (New York: Paperback Library, 1972).

John Goodbody wrote *The Illustrated History of Gymnastics* (New York: Beaufort Books, 1983).

William I. Grossman wrote *A Primer of Gross Pathology* (Springfield, IL: Thomas, 1972).

Roger Grounds wrote *The Perfect Lawn* (London: Ward Lock, 1974).

Norman Knight wrote *Chess Pieces* (London: Sampson Low, 1949).

A. Lord wrote *The Grace of God* (Truro, UK: James R. Netherton, 1859).

G. A. Martini wrote *Metabolic Changes Induced by Alcohol* (Berlin: Springer Verlag, 1971).

L. G. Chiozza Money wrote *Riches and Poverty* (London: Methuen, 1908).

Jack Roy Strange wrote *Abnormal Psychology: Understanding Behavior Disorders* (New York: McGraw-Hill, 1965).

Mary Twelveponies wrote *There Are No Problem Horses, Only Problem Riders* (Boston: Houghton Mifflin, 1982).

INSANE REAL BOOK TITLES

How to Shit in the Woods: An Environmentally Sound Approach to a Lost Art, once an international bestseller, the book is a must for all fecal tourists and sylvan defecators.

People Who Don't Know They're Dead, a courageous book about supernatural squatters recalling how Uncle Wally and Aunt Ruth (Wally's sister) came to counsel dead spirits who took up residence in bodies that didn't belong to them.

The Big Book of Lesbian Hair Stories: When These Sapphic Sisters Saddle Up, Ecstasy Is Only a Hoofbeat Away! Eight stories set in different historical periods involving women, horses, and forbidden love.

You Are Worthless, a book that will help you overcome struggles with self-esteem by giving you permission to acknowledge your true worthlessness.

How to Avoid Huge Ships, a book about a problem that just doesn't seem to go away.

Whose Bottom Is This? This book teaches children about wild animals by displaying color photographs of hippo butts, rhino butts, bighorn sheep butts, and pintailed duck butts and then displaying the entire animals on the next page. A book that asks the question, "Whose butt is it, anyway?"

Bombproof Your Horse, a book teaching equestrians how to produce safe, tractable, and pleasurable mounts.

Better Never to Have Been: The Harm of Coming into Existence, a timely, uplifting book on the virtues of nonreproduction and extinction, reminding one of Schopenhauer, who said that it is a sin to be born and that to desire immortality is to desire the eternal perpetuation of a great mistake.

Castration: The Advantages and the Disadvantages, a book with balls—for now.

I Was Tortured by the Pygmy Love Queen, a book about a U.S. Navy fighter pilot who was forced to abandon his plane and to parachute into a rain forest canopy, where he was greeted by a lost tribe of pygmies and their insanely cruel leader.

Cheese Problems Solved, a timely book that has the courage to answer more than 200 questions about cheese and the entire cheese-making process.

Circumcisions by Appointment: Life in Eighteenth Century Manchester, a book whose title says it all.

Reusing Old Graves, a book that teaches us that there's always room for more.

Italian without Words, a book that teaches readers to speak perfect Italian completely through eloquent Italian gestures, engaging not only the mind but also the fingers.

Living with Crazy Buttocks, a book describing absurdities of contemporary culture, taking a long, hard look at not only Barbara Cartland's beauty secrets but also Ricky Martin's bottom.

The Pyramid Scheme: How to Use Friends to Build Your Empire, a book with wise advice for the age of Madoff.

The Joy of Uncircumcising, a book that has raised quite a flap, especially among our male members.

The Beginner's Guide to Sex in the Afterlife, a book that discusses sexual energies that are imperceptible to physical eyes and paints the sexual big picture, teaching us that death needn't put a crimp in our sex lives.

What's Your Poo Telling You, a book with a brown cover illustrating more than two dozen "dookies," including The Floater, The Log Jam, The Glass Shard, The Déjà Poo, and The Hanging Chad; great bathroom reading, the book combines accurate descriptions with medical advice, useful for everyone—not just gastroenterologists and their brownnosers.

The Stray Shopping Carts of Eastern North America: A Guide to Field Identification, a book that teaches us manic consumers that life isn't all about us; it's also about our shopping conveyances.

CHAPTER 36

The Shoe Polish Is Not Italian but Polish: Capitonyms

Capitonyms are words that change their meaning and pronunciation when they are capitalized. The word comes from *capital* and the suffix *-onym* (name, word). They are often treated as heteronyms—that is, as words spelled the same but having different pronunciations and meanings, except that capitonyms, by definition, involve uppercase letters.

Ares (AIR-eez) = the Greek god of war
ares (airs) = multiple units of 100 square units
Askew (AS-kew) = Reubin Askew, governor of Florida in the 1970s
askew (uh-SKEW) = to one side; crooked
August (AW-guhst) = the eighth month
august (aw-GUHST) = magnificent
Begin (BEG-in) = the Israeli prime minister of the 1970s and the 1980s
begin (buh-GIN) = to start
Degas (duh-GAH) = French painter
degas (dee-GAS) = to remove gas from

Embarrass (AUM-broh) = a river in eastern Illinois

embarrass (em-BAR[BER]-uhs) = humiliate

Ewe (AY-way) = a member of a people inhabiting Ghana, southeast Ghana, southern Togo, and southern Benin

ewe (yoo) = a female sheep

Herb (hurb) = nickname for Herbert

herb (urb) = a plant or plant part valued for its medicinal, savory, or aromatic qualities

Job (johb) = a book and character in the Bible

job (jahb) = a piece of work, a task, or an occupation

Lima (LEE-muh) = the capital of Peru

lima (LY-muh) = a bean

Magdalen (MAWD-len) = a college in Oxford University

magdalen (MAG-duh-len) = a reformed prostitute; a refuge or reformatory for prostitutes

Male (MAH-lee) = the capital of the Maldives

male (mayl) = the opposite of female

Millet (Mi-LAY) = Jean-François Millet, French painter

millet (MIL-uht) = a cereal

Mobile (Moh-BEEL) = a seaport in Alabama

mobile (MOH-buhl) = capable of moving steadily

Natal (na-TAHL) = a region of southeast Africa

natal (NAYD-uhl): pertaining to birth

Nestlé (NES-lee): the famous corporation

nestle (NES-uhl) = settle snugly

Nice (neese) = a port in southeastern France

nice (nys) = pleasant

Rainier (ray-NEER) = a volcanic peak in the state of Washington

rainier (RANE-ee-uhr) = more rainy

Reading (RED-ing) = a city in southeastern Pennsylvania

reading (REE-ding) = the act of recognizing and understanding written language

Tangier (tan-JEER) = a seaport in northern Morocco

tangier (TANG-ee-uhr) = more tangy

Worms (Vorms) = a city in southwest Germany

worms (wurms) = soft-bodied crawling animals

CHAPTER 37

When We Were Robbed in a Copse, We Called the Cops: Homophones

The word *homophone* comes from the Greek-derived *hom-* (same) and *-phone* (sound, voice). A homophone is a word that is pronounced the same as another but differs in meaning, such as *rose* (flower) and *rose* (past tense of *rise*). Homophones can have the same spelling but they needn't, as in *carat* and *carrot*. Here are some obscure homophones of some common words.

answer	anser (*genus of birds containing geese*)
braille	brail (*one of several small ropes attached to the leech of a sail for drawing the sail in or up*)
cops	copse (*thicket or growth of small trees*)
crewmen	crumen (*the tear bag or suborbital gland in deer and antelope*)
crisis	chrysis (*genus of brilliantly colored wasps*)
cross	crosse (*stick used in game of lacrosse*)

duke	dook (*an incline at a mine for hauling*)
fade	fayed (*fit closely as timbers in shipbuilding*)
file	phial (*small container of liquids, especially medicine*)
furs	furze (*spiny evergreen shrub common throughout Europe*)
glare	glair (*a liquid made from egg white*)
groin	groyne (*barrier against the tide to prevent beach erosion*)
impressed	imprest (*a loan or advance of money*)
ingrain	engrain (*to color in imitation of a wood's grain*)
lewd	leud (*feudal tenant in the ancient Frankish kingdoms*)
liter	lieder (*German folk songs*)
meddler	medlar (*a Eurasian tree*)
mere	mir (*prerevolutionary Russian peasant commune*)
moolah	mullah (*learned teacher of the laws and dogmas of Islam*)
oppressed	appressed (*pressed close*)
poem	pome (*fleshy fruit with a central core and usually five seeds, such as an apple*)
police	pelisse (*furred long cloak with arm openings*)
random	randem (*three horses harnessed, one behind the other, to a vehicle*)
send	scend (*to heave upward under the influence of a natural force, as a ship on a wave*)

| shot | chott (*shallow saline lake of northern Africa*) |

A CHORUS OF HOMOPHONES: WORDS WITH MULTIPLE HOMOPHONES

AIR

aire = person of any rank in early Irish Society above the common freeman and below the king

are = 100 square meters

Ayr = city in Scotland

e'er = contraction of *ever*

ere = sooner than, before, previous

eyr = obsolete for *air*

eyre = itinerant judge who rode a circuit to hold court in different counties in England

heir = beneficiary, inheritor

SIGH

psi = twenty-third letter of the Greek alphabet

scye = armhole's shape or outline

sie = dialectal in Britain for *sink, fall, descend*

SOLE

soal = British for a dirty pond; obsolete for the sole of a shoe

sol = a coin and monetary unit of Peru; the fifth tone of the diatonic musical scale

sole = underpart of shoe, boot, foot

soul = essence, principle of life, spirit

soule = obsolete spelling of *soul*
sowl = to pull by the ears
sowle = variant spelling of *soul*

WHEEL
weal = profit, prosperity, well-being
weel = obsolete for *whirlpool*
wele = happiness; prosperity
we'll = contraction of *we will* or *we shall*
wheal = pimple, pustule

CHAPTER 38

You Can't Have Only
a Partial Shebang:
One-Trick Words

Just as some ponies in a circus may be used for only one trick (one-trick ponies), so a word may be always or nearly always used in only one phrase. Sometimes words survive only in idioms. Sometimes the idioms describe unique phenomena, as in *arms akimbo*. At other times, the idioms preserve words that are usually replaced by more common synonyms, as when people refer to fitting or deserved punishment as *condign punishment*.

one is taken **aback**
aid and **abet**
far or farther **afield**
with malice **aforethought**
self-**aggrandizing**
arms **akimbo**
make **amends**
run **amok**
anecdotal evidence
look **askance**

cast **aspersions**

anchors **aweigh**

bald-faced lie

bandied about

bated breath

be-all and end-all

beck and call

bedside manner

betwixt and between

bogged down

in **cahoots**

champing at the bit

cheesed off

old **codger**

got his or her **comeuppance**

condign punishment

nook and **cranny**

crick in the neck

dandle on one's knee

just **deserts**

by **dint** of

dolled up

dribs and drabs

if I had my **druthers**

a word in **edgeways**

eke out

extenuating circumstances

figment of the imagination

a **fine-tooth** comb

fobbed off

Heaven **forfend**

on the **fritz**

to and **fro**

gainfully employed

gird one's loins
grist for the mill
gung ho
gussied up
halcyon days
hale and hearty
hem and **haw**
hem and haw
hunker down
time **immemorial**
indomitable will
make or made **inroads**
to all **intents** and purposes
the **jig** is up
keeling over
kith and kin
death **knell**
in **lieu** of
at **loggerheads**
filthy **lucre**
far from the **madding** crowd
moot point
much of a **muchness**
in the **offing**
noised abroad
opposable thumbs
overreach oneself
hoist with one's own **petard**
peter out
pomp and circumstance
on the **QT**
raring to go
rue the day
runcible spoon

scantily clad
scrimp and save
serried ranks
whole **shebang**
shored up
slake one's thirst
sleight of hand
spick and span
various and **sundry**
tabby cat
tit for **tat**
on **tenterhooks**
toeing the line
trials and **tribulations**
in a **trice**
moral **turpitude**
ulterior motive(s)
take **umbrage** at
vale of tears
vantage point
vested interest
vim and vigor
make the **welkin** ring
whiling away
young **whippersnapper**
wishful thinking
wreak havoc
zoot suit

CHAPTER 39

Welsh Rabbit Is a Cheese Dish: Misnomers, Misleading Expressions, and Illogicalities

Many misconceptions come from taking expressions literally without understanding the context from which they arose. For example, *Welsh rabbit* describes a cheese dish whose name relates to the belief that poor Welsh citizens couldn't afford meat. In short, the expression is ironic. Similarly, the expression *black box* to describe a recording device on large airplanes is related to death and destruction but doesn't relate to the color of the device, which is orange, to make it conspicuous among wreckage. *Panama hats* were shipped first to Panama before being shipped to other continents, but they originated in Ecuador. For more on misconceptions, you may want to pick up my book *Sorry, Wrong Answer*.

Other misleading expressions come from inattention, as when apathetic people describe their apathy as a mental state in which they *could care less* when they mean "couldn't care less." Other expressions come from words that originally described things that have changed over time. Chalkboards were black and hence were called blackboards, but many of them came to be green or blue, and now they have been largely displaced by white boards, which require special erasable markers.

There is no butter in buttermilk.
Blackboards can be blue or green.
Black boxes on large airplanes are orange.
Peanuts aren't peas or nuts; they're legumes.
English muffins weren't invented in England but in America.
French poodles originated in Germany.
French fries weren't invented in France but in Belgium.
Danish pastries aren't from Denmark but Austria.
Hot water heaters are simply water heaters.
The second hand on a watch is the third hand.
Tugboats should only pull rather than push.
Mobile homes got the name from the name of the place where they were first mass produced: Mobile, Alabama.
The Norway rat originated in North China.
Hollandaise sauce originated in France.
Dutch clocks originated in Germany.
Chinese checkers can be traced to a nineteenth-century English game called Halma.
Great Danes originated in Germany.
Russian dressing was invented in the United States.
A jackrabbit is a hare.
A Belgian hare is a rabbit.
The monkey wrench was named after Charles Moncky.
A male purple finch is crimson, and a female purple finch is brown-gray flecked.

The official name of the world's largest train station isn't Grand Central Station but Grand Central Terminal.

Pennsylvania wasn't named after its founder, William Penn (1644–1718), but after his father, Sir William Penn (1621–1670).

The English horn isn't English and isn't a horn but is an alto oboe, a woodwind with an angled mouthpiece. The word *English* mistranslates a French word for "angled."

A horned toad is a lizard.

Bloodhounds are so named not because of their special ability to smell blood but because they were the first breed of dog whose blood or breeding records were maintained.

Jordan almonds originated in Spain.

The Harlem Globetrotters began in Chicago.

Although Venetian blinds were popular in Venice, they originated in Japan, where they were made of bamboo.

India ink is from China.

Arabic numerals are from India.

Brown bears aren't always brown but can be white, cream, brown, cinnamon, and blue.

Greyhounds aren't always grey (or gray) but can be white, black, and other colors.

Fireflies aren't flies but beetles.

A guinea pig is not a pig or from Guinea but a South American rodent.

A titmouse isn't a mouse but a bird.

Happy hours and rush hours can last longer than sixty minutes.

Quicksand works slowly.

Boxing rings are square.

Welsh rabbit is a cheese dish.

When people say that they could care less, they mean they couldn't care less.

When people say that someone wants to have his cake and eat it too (an everyday occurrence), they mean that someone wants to eat his cake and have it too (an impossibility).

When people say that they really miss not seeing you, they mean that they miss seeing you.

When people say that the movie kept them literally glued to their seats or something had them literally climbing the walls, they don't mean what they say.

A near miss is a near hit.

Things don't really fall between the cracks but through the cracks.

People don't cross bridges but whatever is under the bridges and perpendicular to the bridges.

Doughnut holes aren't holes but what fills them.

Announcements aren't made by nameless officials but by unnamed officials.

People can't put their best foot forward, only the better one.

Although people are told to keep a stiff upper lip, it is, as Richard Lederer and other authors have pointed out, the lower one that quivers when people are emotional.

When people do things behind your back, they have no choice because they can't do things in front of your back.

When people say that someone has a self-deprecating (self-disapproving) sense of humor, they mean a self-depreciating (self-belittling) sense of humor.

The Canary Islands weren't named after canary birds but after dogs, the extinct race of large dogs (Latin

Canis) that once roamed there. The bird is named after the Canary Islands.

Technically, there is no such thing as the Congressional Medal of Honor. It is the Medal of Honor, though it is presented "in the name of the Congress of the United States."

CHAPTER 40

My Acoustic Guitar Was Just a Guitar Before the Invention of Electric Guitars: Retronyms

Retronyms are adjective–noun pairings made necessary by a change in a noun's meaning, usually because of technology. For example, what used to be called *books* (which always had hard covers) are now called hardcover books to distinguish them from paperback books.

acoustic guitar	created because of the invention of electric guitars
AM radio	created when FM radio was introduced
analog watch	created when digital watches were introduced
bar soap	created to distinguish it from liquid or gel soap

black-and-white television	created to distinguish it from color television
cloth diaper	created after the invention of disposable diapers
Coca-Cola Classic	created when the original recipe was introduced after New Coke failed to catch on
conventional oven	created after the invention of the microwave oven
corn on the cob	created after the introduction of canned corn
disposable battery	created after rechargeable batteries became popular
film camera	created after the invention of digital cameras
George H. W. Bush	became popular only after George W. Bush became president, before which time George (H. W.) Bush rarely if ever used his middle initials
LED mouse	created after the invention of the laser mouse
Original Recipe chicken	created to distinguish the original Kentucky Fried Chicken from Extra Crispy chicken and other varieties

Orthodox Judaism	created after the introduction of Reform and Conservative movements
paleoconservative	created after the development of neoconservatism
regular coffee	created after the invention of decaffeinated coffee

CHAPTER 41

You'll Find Phoenicians in Phoenix: Domunyms

Go to Norfolk, Virginia, and you'll see Norfolkians; go to Norfolk, Nebraska, and you'll see Norfolkans; go to Norfolk, England, and you'll see neither Norfolkians nor Norfolkans but North Anglians. Consider some unexpected domunyms, which identify people from a particular place.

Aberdonians	Aberdeen, Scotland; Aberdeen, South Dakota; Aberdeen, Washington
Accidentals	Accident, Maryland
Allentonians	Allentown, Pennsylvania
Arkansas Citians	Arkansas City, Arkansas
Atlantic Cityites	Atlantic City, New Jersey
Beirutis	Beirut, Lebanon
Cantabrigians (or Cantabridgians)	Cambridge, England; Cambridge, Massachusetts
Charles Towners	Charles Town, West Virginia

Townies	Charlestown, Massachusetts
Cestrians	Chester or Chesire, England
Corpus Christians	Corpus Christi, Texas
Darbians (or Darbyites)	Derbyshire, England
Exonians	Exeter, England
Florentines	Florence, Italy
Fort Scotters	Fort Scott, Kansas
Fort Waynites	Fort Wayne, Indiana
Fort Worthians (or Fort Worthers)	Fort Worth, Texas
Frederictonians	Frederick, Maryland
Dismalites	Great Dismal Swamp, Virginia and North Carolina
Greensburghers	Greensboro, North Carolina
Hamburgers	Hamburg, Germany
Manxmen, Manxwomen	Island of Man
Jeffersonians	Jeffersontown, Kentucky
Liverpudlans	Liverpool, England
Chunkers	Mauch Chunk, Pennsylvania
Hatters	Medicine Hat, Alberta
Moscowites	Moscow, Idaho
Neapolitans	Naples, Italy
Delhites	New Delhi, India

Plainsmen, Plainswomen	Plains, Georgia
Punxyites	Punxsutawney, Pennsylvania
Qataris	Qatar
Richmondites	Richmond, California/ Indiana
Richmonders	Richmond, Virginia
Rochesterites	Rochester, Indiana
Rochesterians	Rochester, New York
Rocky Mounters	Rocky Mount, North Carolina
Cruzans	Saint Croix, Virgin Islands
Saratogians	Saratoga Springs, New York
Tangerines	Tangier, Morocco
Cythereans (from the Latin)	Venus

CHAPTER 42

Calling All Mouse Potatoes: Neologisms

Neologisms are newly coined words or expressions. Sometimes neologisms vanish shortly after they are created. Whether a neologism sticks around depends on several factors, not least the extent to which it is quickly accepted by the public. Rarely will a word enter common usage unless it fairly clearly resembles other words.

Sometimes neologisms come directly from popular literature or are popularized there. Accordingly, *grok* (to achieve complete intuitive understanding) comes from Robert A. Heinlein's *Stranger in a Strange Land*; *McJob*, coined by sociologist Amitai Etzioni on August 24, 1986, in a *Washington Post* article, was popularized by Douglas Coupland in his *Generation X: Tales for an Accelerated Culture*. *Cyberspace* comes from William Gibson's book *Neuromancer*. Sometimes the title of a book becomes a neologism, as in Joseph Heller's *Catch-22*, which describes a no-win situation. At other times, neologisms are inspired by the names of authors, especially when the authors are associated with a particular style (*Kafkaesque*, which describes surreal distortion often accompanied by a sense of impending danger) or a particular work (*Orwellian*, which describes the dehumanizing manipulation and systemic dishonesty of a totalitarian state, as in George Orwell's novel *1984*). Lewis Carroll has been called "the king of neologistic poems" because of his poem "Jabberwocky," which includes dozens of invented words, such as *bandersnatch* (a swift fierce wild animal), *brillig* (four o'clock in the afternoon), and *chortle* (a combination of *chuckle* and *snort*).

The following list contains colorful expressions that have gained currency within the last few years.

baggervation = the feeling one gets at an airport when other travelers have found their luggage but one hasn't

beehacker = a beekeeper who uses digital technology to monitor and manage hives

butler lie = a lie used to politely avoid or end an e-mail, instant message, or phone call

cheapuccino = inexpensive, inferior cappuccino usually bought from a vending machine

elderburbia = suburbs with a predominantly elderly population

gate rape = phrase for pat downs by the TSA (Transportation Security Administration) at airports

hathos = feelings of pleasure from hating someone or something

juvenoia = a baseless and exaggerated fear that the Internet and social trends are having seriously negative effects on children

mouse potato = someone who spends an excessive amount of time on a computer

nom de womb = unborn child whose expectant parents don't want to know his or her sex before birth paperphilia = a preference for reading material that is on paper and not on a computer screen; those individuals are paperphiles.

pity friend = on a social networking site, a person whose friend request you accept out of pity

quiet party = a party in which talking (beyond whispering) and loud noises are prohibited and in which guests communicate using handwritten notes; whispering (in designated areas) is allowed

silent soccer = soccer in which spectators are seen but not heard and in which they aren't permitted to yell, cheer, or coach from the sidelines

singlism = workplace discrimination against unmarried employees; the negative stereotyping of unmarried people

skyaking = jumping out of planes with one's kayak

smirting = flirting while outside a building to smoke

soul patch = small growth of beard under a man's lower lip

spillionaire = a person who got rich because of the British Petroleum oil spill in the Gulf of Mexico

starting marriage = short, first marriage and divorce ending with no children, no property, and no regrets

talking hairdo = a TV journalist who is superficial or who values appearance over substance

tombstoning = jumping or diving into water from a dangerously high perch, such as a tall bridge

CHAPTER 43

Words Not of This World (or *Any* World): The Alienans

Alienans is a medieval term for an adjective that cancels a noun it qualifies; in effect, an alienans creates the contrary of the word it precedes or at least raises doubts about whether the word it precedes is appropriate. Accordingly, a *fake* doctor is not a doctor, and an *alleged* doctor may not be, and sometimes isn't, a doctor. Each of the following words can function as an alienans:

alleged
birthday (as in *birthday suit*)
bogus
counterfeit
decoy
fake
mock
phony

NATIONAL EPITHETS

The word *Dutch* can also function as an alienans, as in *Dutch treat*, which doesn't describe a treat but describes each person's paying his or her own way. In fact, most slang expressions with the word *Dutch* are unflattering to the Dutch, who once competed against the English for control of the seas.

There are other unflattering, indeed prejudiced, ethnic epithets, each functioning as an alienans, such as *French* (as in *French faith*, which once meant "faithlessness"), *Irish* (as in *Irish dinner*, which can mean "nothing to eat"), and *Scotch* (as in *Scotch rabbit*, which, like *Welsh rabbit*, refers not to rabbit but to a meatless cheese dish, supposedly for people who cannot afford meat).

CHAPTER 44

Some Ain't What They Used to Be: Words with Changed Meanings

Words are alive. They are born; they often change, and they sometimes die. Sometimes the meanings of words have changed so much that they can now be used to describe the opposite of what they originally described. As you'll see, *girl* used to refer to a boy or a maiden.

Sometimes words change by having added meanings, as when technology led us to use the word *mouse* to describe a computer device. At other times, words undergo pejoration—that is, they acquire negative meanings. The word *gang*, in an early usage, described a group of workers, but it has come often to be associated with a group of people engaged in criminal or other antisocial activity. Similarly, the word *artificial* used to mean "full of artistic or technical skill."

Sometimes words can come to describe something contrary to their original meanings through their association with similar-looking or similar-sounding words. Although *auburn* today describes what is reddish brown or chestnut colored, it can be traced to Latin *albus* (white). *Auburn* came to English meaning "yellowish white, flaxen" but shifted in the sixteenth century to its current sense of "reddish brown" because of the influence of Middle English *brun* (brown), which also changed its spelling.

awful: The word once meant "full of awe, awe-inspiring" and could describe very good things. Now it usually means "terrible."

banquet: Although the word carried its present meaning as early as the fifteenth century, it did mean for a short time "slight repast between meals" or "snack"— hardly a feast. Accordingly, in 1620, Tobias Venner wrote of "banquets between meals, when the stomach is empty."

blouse: In the nineteenth century, the word could denote a man's shirt, or smock-frock, like the blue smock of French workers. That garment, however, came to be worn by women about 1870, when it was worn as a tunic, and it has remained popular ever since.

bruise: The original meaning of the verb implied a breaking of the skin, and as late as 1755 was defined by lexicographer Samuel Johnson as "crush or mangle."

bully: In the sixteenth century, the word meant "a sweetheart" or "fine fellow." Accordingly, Shakespeare has a character in *Henry V* say: "I love the lovely bully." The term came to have its current sense by association with swashbucklers and hired ruffians.

chuckle: Although the word now describes a soft, subdued laugh, it described vehement laughter in the sixteenth century and was thus defined in Dr. Johnson's dictionary in 1755.

girl: In the thirteenth century, a *girl* could denote a "youth," whether a boy or a maiden. To prevent possible ambiguity, people would usually refer to a boy as a *knave girl*. The word *girls* usually meant "children." The current use of *girl* dates from the sixteenth century.

glamor: The word was originally a synonym for "grammar."

governor: The word once meant "steersman."

idiot: Although many of us today believe that idiots are disproportionately represented in public office, ancient Greeks would use the term—from the root *idios* (private)—to designate those who didn't hold public office. Because such people were regarded as having no special skill or status, the word gradually fell into disrepute (underwent pejoration).

knight: The word once meant "a boy."

let: In Elizabethan times, the word meant "to prevent," as in Hamlet's words, "By heaven, I'll make a ghost of him that lets me," and as in the old legal expression, "without let or hindrance."

lord: The word once meant "loaf giver."

marshal: The word once meant "house servant."

mere: The word originally meant "done alone," as when a person was accused of doing something of his *mere notion*. In the sixteenth century, the word came to carry almost opposite meanings, carrying not only its current meaning (nothing more or better than what is specified) but also the meaning "in the fullest sense," so that a *mere cook* could mean "a perfect cook." Accordingly, Richard Hooker's *Of the Lawes of Ecclesiasticall Politie* refers to the "meer [absolute] Unity" of God.

passenger: In the fourteenth century, the word, which literally means "one who is passing," was used to refer to any traveler, often one on foot. Although the current sense arose in the sixteenth century, the word was used in its "pedestrian" sense as late as the nineteenth century, when Sir Walter Scott wrote in *The Fair Maid of Perth*: "She avoided the High Street . . . and reached the wynd by the narrow lanes. . . . Even those comparatively lonely passages were now astir with passengers."

poison: Literally meaning "potion," the word has the same origin as *potion*. When *poison* came into our language from French in the thirteenth century, it was a potion—that is, a medicine. The word did, however, soon come to refer to a potion or medicine that had been doctored by the addition of a dangerous or deadly drug. From its association with what had been dangerously doctored, *poison* came to carry its current meaning.

prestige: The word once meant "trickery."

restive: Although the word now means "not wanting to rest" and "uneasy," in the seventeenth century it meant "wanting to rest," "not wishing to move," and "inactive."

squire: The word once meant "shield bearer."

stink: From about the thirteenth to the eighteenth centuries, the word was used to describe both sweet and foul smells. The word, however, came to describe only bad smells, so that one could no longer speak of "a good stink." Noah Webster was so much offended by the word *stink* that he deleted it from the Bible, which he translated in 1833.

thrift: The word meant in the thirteenth century "thriving condition" and later "prosperity." Because of its association with "gains" and "savings," it came to carry its current sense of "economic management," which arose in the sixteenth century. The word had shifted its meaning from wealth (an end) to the economy needed to gain wealth (a means).

with: The word once meant—you may not believe this—"against." In Old English, *with* denoted opposition, producing the following paradoxical-sounding idioms: *compete with, contend with, fight with, quarrel with,* and *struggle with.* The Old English word for the current meaning of *with* was *mid* (comparable to modern German *mit*). In the twelfth or thirteenth century *with* lost its "against" meaning and acquired the meaning of the Old English *mid.* Because of its older meaning, alive in expressions such as *fight with,* the word *with* is a contronym, carrying contrary or opposite meanings.

CHAPTER 45

Order Out of Chaos: Literordinyms

This chapter contains English words with three or sometimes four consecutive alphabetical letters, such as *GHI*. Although some three-letter alphabetical sequences are common (such as *DEF*), some are almost unheard of (such as *XYZ*).

ABCoulomb
DEFine
cou**GHI**ng
HIJack
so**MNO**lent
gy**MNOP**hobia
fi**RST**
ove**RSTU**ff
STUpid
hydro**XYZ**ine

Note that some words contain three-letter sequences that are in reverse alphabetical order:

FEDeral
JIHad
cou**PON**
pean**UTS**

CHAPTER 46

The Longest Word: Outlandish Sesquipedalianism

Although millions of Americans love to supersize food and like bigness in many things, we often have mixed feelings about big words. Sometimes we like them, especially when we know them, and most other people don't. At other times, we think that they are pretentious, as when people call an indoor swimming pool a natatorium. In any event, there is no easy answer to the question, What is the longest word in English?

Sometimes words are made up just for show, as when Everett M. Smith, the president of the National Puzzlers' League, created *pneumonoultramicroscopicsilicovolcanoconiosis* to describe a lung disease contracted from inhaling fine silica particles from a volcano. That forty-five-letter word appears to do no more work than that done by the word *silicosis*. In any event, the *Oxford English Dictionary* (*OED*) describes Mr. Smith's coinage as "factitious," requiring some readers to make an extra trip to the dictionary.

The longest word in *Gould's Medical Dictionary* is *hepaticocholangiocholecystenterostomies*, describing surgeries in which surgeons create a connection between the gallbladder and a hepatic bile duct and between the intestine and the gallbladder.

The longest English word in a movie, at least in a famous movie, is *supercalifragilisticexpialidocious*, "even though the sound of it is something quite atrocious." The word is from Walt Disney's *Mary Poppins* (where it is also the title of a song), and its meaning, to the extent that it has one, is vague though positive. In the movie we're told that you should use the word when "you don't know what to say." Mary Poppins uses the word when she has nothing else to say upon winning a horse race. According to Richard M. Sherman, cowriter of the song introducing the word, the word was created mostly out of double-talk. In 1965, the song was the subject of an unsuccessful lawsuit by songwriters Gloria Parker and Barney Young, who argued that it was a copyright infringement of their 1951 song called "Supercalafajalistickespeealadojus." The plaintiffs lost their case at least partly because affidavits were produced showing that variants of the word were known long before the 1951 song. In any event, the word *supercalifragilisticexpialidocious* has roots that have been defined as *super-* (above), *cali-* (beauty), *fragilistic-* (delicate), *expiali-* (to atone), and *docious-* (educable), yielding, roughly, through the sum of its parts, "atoning for extreme and delicate beauty [while being] highly educable."

The longest word in the first edition of the *OED* is *floccinaucinihilipilification*, which curiously lacks the most common English letter, *E*, but which compensates for that deficiency by containing the letter *I* nine times. Meaning "estimating something as worthless" and dating back to 1741, the word is described as the longest *real* word in the *OED* by the 1992 *Guinness Book of World Records*, which describes *pneumonoultramicroscopicsilicovolcanokoniosis* as the longest made-up English word.

Perhaps the most popular English word in recent decades simply because of its length is *antidisestablishmentarianism*, which originally described the political position of being opposed to stopping the Church of England from continuing to be the official church of England, Ireland, and Wales, though the term has been used to describe a political philosophy opposed to the separation of religion and government.

The longest word in Shakespeare is *honorificabilitudinitatibus*, which means "the state of being able to achieve honor" and which appears in Shakespeare's *Love's Labour's Lost* (act V, scene 1). In 1721, it was listed by *Bailey's Dictionary* as the longest word in English. It is also one of the longest English words with alternating consonants and vowels.

The two longest words in *Merriam-Webster's Collegiate Dictionary* (tenth edition) are *electroencephalographically* and *ethylenediaminetetraacetate*.

The longest English words in common usage, according to the 1992 *Guinness Book of World Records* are *disproportionableness* and *incomprehensibilities*.

Two of ten 100-letter words created by James Joyce in *Finnegans Wake* are *babababadalgharaghtakamminarronnkonnbronntonnerronntuonnthunntrovarrhounawnskawntoohoohoordenenthurnuk*, which means "a symbolic thunderclap that represents the fall of Adam and Eve," and *klikkaklakkaklaskaklopatzklatschabattacreppycrottygraddaghsemmihsammihnouithappluddyappladdypkonpkot*, which represents the sound of crashing glass. The first-mentioned word is on the first page of *Finnegans Wake*.

It is possible to create words that are tediously long and that no one would use except to mention examples of words that are tediously long. As Paul Hellweg says in *The Insomniac Dictionary: The Last Word on the Odd Word*, it is possible to create run-on words that are nauseatingly long, as by stretching out the term "great-great-great-great-great-great-great grandfather (or mother)" 100,000 or more times. That activity and its results would, however, be excruciatingly boring. Similarly, people could create artificial terms to describe complex chemical compounds. People could create chemical words with thousands of letters, but such creations haven't been used and wouldn't be used by chemists, who use chemical notation to simplify and abbreviate information. True, some extremely large agglutinative (glued-together) terms for complex chemical compounds have been used by chemists. In the American Chemical Society's *Chemical Abstracts*, the following 1,185-letter name for tobacco mosaic virus, Dahlemense strain has appeared: *acetylseryltyrosylserylisoleucylthreonylserylprolylserylglutaminylphenylalanylvalylphenylalanylleucylserylserylvalyltryptophylalanylaspartylprolylisoleucylglutamylleucylleucylasparaginylvalylcysteinylthreonylserylserylleucylglycylasparaginylglutaminylphenylalanylglutaminylthreonylglutaminylglutaminylalanylarginylthreonylthreonylglutaminylvalylglutaminylglutaminylphenylalanylserylglutaminylvalyltryptophyllysylprolylphenylalanylprolylglutaminylserylthreonylvalylarginylphenylalanylprolylglycylaspartylvalyltyrosyllysylvalyltyrosylarginyltyrosylasparaginylalanylvalylleucylaspartylprolylleucyliso-*

leucylthreonylalanylleucylleucylglycylthreonylphenylal-
anylaspartylthreonylarginylasparaginylarginyliso-
leucylisoleucylglutamylvalylglutamylasparaginylgluta-
minylglutaminylserylprolylthreonylthreonylalanylglu-
tamylthreonylleucylaspartylalanylthreonylarginylargi-
nylvalylaspartylaspartylalanylthreonylvalylalanyliso-
leucylarginylserylalanylasparaginylisoleucylasparagin-
ylleucylvalylasparaginylglutamylleucylvalylarginylgly-
cylthreonylglycylleucyltyrosylasparaginylglutaminylas-
paraginylthreonylphenylalanylglutamylserylmethionyl-
serylglycylleucylvalyltryptophylthreonylserylalanylp-
rolylalanylserine. (Fortunately, the molecule can be
succinctly expressed in the formula $C_{785}H_{1220}N_{212}O_{248}S_2$.)

In short, although we can determine with certainty
the longest defined term (definiendum) in any particular dictionary, we have no way to answer the largely
unqualified question, What is the longest word in English? One thing is certain. Whatever word one selects
will be a word that is rarely if ever used.

CHAPTER 47

Changing Black to White the Easy Way: Word Chains

We can change one word into a contrary or even an opposite word in sometimes just a few steps by changing one letter at a time, as we change *black* into *white*. Although verbal transformations involving only a few steps (*lead* to *gold*, for example) are easy, those involving several steps require a good deal of ingenuity or trial and error.

WE CAN CHANGE *BLACK* TO *WHITE*:
black
blank
blink
clink
chink
chine
whine
white

WE CAN CHANGE *LEAD* INTO *GOLD*:
lead
load

goad
gold

WE CAN CHANGE *LESS* TO *MORE*:
less
Tess
toss
moss
most
Mort
more

WE CAN CHANGE *DOG* TO *CAT*:
dog
cog
cot
cat

WE CAN CHANGE *FIND* TO *LOSE*:
find
fine
line
lone
lose

WE CAN CHANGE *GIVE* TO *TAKE*:
give
live
like
lake
take

WE CAN CHANGE *HEAD* TO *TAIL*:
head
heal

ROD L. EVANS

teal
tell
tall
tail

WE CAN CHANGE *HATE* TO *LOVE*:
hate
rate
rave
cave
cove
love

WE CAN CHANGE *POOR* TO *RICH*:
poor
boor
book
rook
rock
Rick
rich

WE CAN CHANGE *TEARS* TO *SMILE*:
tears
sears
stars
stare
stale
stile
smile

CHAPTER 48

Bohemians Are Usually Not from Bohemia: Words Derived from Place Names

Many words gain their descriptive power from their association with place names. Sometimes things are named after their place of origin, as in the case of Angora cats, named after Angora, a variant and former name of Ankara, Turkey. The geopolitical term *balkanization*, now considered pejorative, originally described the process by which a region or state becomes fragmented into hostile factions. The term was originally inspired by new states that arose from the collapse of the Austro-Hungarian Empire and the Russian Empire.

Industries or professions are often described by places or streets with which they are associated. Accordingly, *Broadway* is often used to describe musical theater; *Madison Avenue* has described the advertising industry; *Fleet Street* has been used to describe the British press because it is a London street that used to house many newspapers.

The following list contains words inspired by place names:

bedlam (*pandemonium*):   after a popular name and pronunciation of St. Mary of Bethlehem, London's first psychiatric hospital

bikini (*skimpy two-piece bathing suit*):   after Bikini Atoll in the Marshal Islands, where atomic bombs were tested in 1946—supposedly analogous to the explosive effect on the male libido

boeotian (*a pejorative for "stupid"*):   after the Boeotian people, who were considered obtuse by many Greeks

bohemian (*describing individuals who wish to live an unconventional lifestyle*):   after Bohemia, where gypsies were erroneously thought to have originated

brummagem (*goods of shoddy quality*):   after a local pronunciation of Birmingham, a city in the United Kingdom once associated with shoddy goods

chautauqua (*a form of local fair*):   after Chautauqua, New York, where a local fair was held

Chinese wall (*artificial organizational barrier*):   after the Great Wall of China

denim (*a coarse cotton fabric*):   after French serge de Nimes, or serge of Nimes, where the cloth originated

donnybrook (*colloquial term for a brawl or fracas*):   after Donnybrook Fair, an annual horse fair in a Dublin suburb notorious for fighting and drunkenness

doolally or dolally (*mad or eccentric*):   after Deolali, the name of a town in India with a military sanatorium and a transit camp

duffel or duffle (*heavy woolen cloth*):   after Duffel, a town in Belgium where the cloth was first made

fez (*a red conical hat*):   after Fez, Morocco

CHAPTER 49

Word Records in the Outer Limits

Some English words are noteworthy not because of their meanings but because of their structure, as when they contain all five regular vowels in alphabetical order, or when they contain alternating consonants and vowels, such as *supererogatorily* (which means "in a manner that is beyond the call of duty"). The words that follow, like *supererogatorily*, go beyond expectations:

abhors, almost, begins, biopsy, chimps, chinos, chintz = Some of the few six-letter words composed of letters that occur in alphabetical order without repetition.

abracadabra = The longest common word with the most repeats of the letter *A*.

abstemious, facetious = The two most common words containing the five regular vowels in alphabetical order. *Abstemious* means "sparing in eating and drinking."

adieu, aerie, audio, eerie, queue = The longest common words with only one consonant.

Aeaeae = The only all-vowel six-letter word. *Aeaeae* is

both a surname of the legendary Circe (who turned men into swine) and a name of a small island off the coast of Italy, where Circe is said to have lived.

aegilops = *Aegilops* (when used as a proper noun) is a genus of wild-oat grass. When the word is used in lowercase, it has described an ulcer or fistula in the inner corner of the eye.

aerious = The shortest word with all five regular vowels in alphabetical order is this seventeenth-century synonym of *aerial*. *Anemious* (of plants, growing in exposed windy places) has one more letter than *aerious* and is so rare as not to be in most dictionaries. Another eight-letter word is *aleikoum*, a word present in the transliteration of the Arabic Muslim salutation *Salaam aleikoum* (May peace be upon you). There are other fairly short words fitting the criteria, such as *arsenious* (pertaining to arsenic) and *parecious* (of plants, having the male and female organs beside or near each other).

aftereffects, desegregated, desegregates, reverberated, stewardesses = Some of the longest words that can be typed using only those letters normally typed with the left hand.

aitch = The spelling of the letter *H* would be pronounced the same after losing the first four letters (see *queue*).

alleluia, assesses, nonunion = The longest common words with only one type of consonant. *Alleluia* is, as it appears to be, a variant of *hallelujah*.

ambidextrously = The longest common word that doesn't repeat any letters (isogram).

antiskepticism = The longest uncommon word with typewriter letters from alternating hands.

aqueuous, mioued, queuing, sequoia = The most common words with the most consecutive vowels. *Mioued* is a variant of *meowed*.

archchronicler, catchphrase, *Eschscholtzia*, Festschrift, Knightsbridge, latchstring, Weltschmerz = All those words contain six consecutive consonants. *Eschscholtzia* is a genus of poppies. *Festschrift* describes a volume of essays by different authors honoring a scholar. *Knightsbridge* is the name of a famous London street and district. *Weltschmerz* describes a sadness from contrasting the actual world with an ideal one.

arched = The longest one-syllable word beginning with the letter *A*.

archfiends = The longest two-syllable word beginning with the letter *A*.

armorial, Concorde (the supersonic airplane), ganymede, mandarin, memorial, mainland = Some of the few common words spellable by concatenating four two-letter state postal codes.

assessee, keelless = The shortest words with three pairs of double letters.

BaLlOoNeD = The longest common alternade, forming *blond* and *aloe* when alternating letters are grouped.

beefily, billowy = The longest common words whose letters are in alphabetical order, with exactly one repeated letter.

Beijing, hijinks, Fiji = The most common words with the most consecutive dotted letters.

boldface, feedback = The shortest words containing all the letters *A* to *F*.

bookkeeper = The best-known word with the most consecutive letter pairs. Richard Lederer and others have advanced *subbookkeeper*, which is listed, for

example, by Urban Dictionary (urbandictionary
.com) and which has been used to describe a person
who works under the direction of the main bookkeeper.

breakthroughs = The longest two-syllable word beginning with the letter *B*.

broughams = The longest one-syllable word beginning
with the letter *B*; it also contains the longest sequence of silent letters in a word (ugha). The -ueue
of *queue*, once removed, leaves a letter, not a word,
and one can argue that one of the *ue* occurrences is
pronounced.

buoyancies, coequality = The shortest (fairly) common
words with the five regular vowels and the letter *Y*
in any order. There are some shorter words, but they
are hard to find outside special dictionaries, such as
medical ones. For example, *euryopia* describes an
abnormally wide opening of the eyes. *Euryomia*
describes groups of beetles related to scarabs. *Pres-
byacousia*, which is in many dictionaries, describes
poor hearing due to aging.

cabbaged, Fabaceae = The longest words whose letters can be played on a musical instrument (piano
words). *Cabbaged*, by the way, is the past tense of
cabbage, which can function as a verb, meaning "to
take surreptitiously or to steal." *Fabaceae* describes
a large plant family comprising the peas, beans, and
related herbaceous or woody plants with pealike
flowers and a legume as fruit.

catchphrase = The most frequently used word containing six consonants in a row.

CHECKBOOK = The longest word composed entirely
of letters with horizontal symmetry in uppercase.
Some other eight-letter words with that property

are *BEDECKED, BOOHOOED, CODEBOOK*, and *COOKBOOK*.

chincherinchee = The only known English word with one letter occurring once, two letters occurring twice, and three letters occurring three times, it describes a southern African perennial bulbous herb.

cimicid = The longest word that consists only of Roman numerals, it describes a bug of the family Cimicidae, which includes bedbugs.

clotheshorse = The longest two-syllable word beginning with the letter *C*.

cockamamie = The longest unaffixed word consisting of only odd letters (that is, the first, third, fifth, seventh letters, etc., of the alphabet).

conservationalists, conversationalists = The longest nonscientific words that are anagrams of each other.

cooee = The shortest word with two double letters. It's chiefly Australian and means "a way to attract attention or give warning."

coueeing, miaouing, queueing = Words with all have five consecutive vowels. *Kauaian*, the usual adjective for "of the Hawaiian island of Kauai" also has five consecutive vowels. *Coueeing* means "making a couee sound," and *miaouing* is a variant of *meowing*.

couscous = *Couscous* is the longest word such that one can't tell visually whether it's been written in all uppercase or all lowercase letters.

crabcake = The only common word containing the *ABC* sequence. Two other words are *dabchick* (which can describe any of several aquatic birds) and *abcoulomb* (which describes a particular electromagnetic unit quantity of electricity).

craunched = The longest one-syllable word beginning with the letter *C*, it means "crunched."

damndest = A variant spelling of *damnedest*, it contains the most consecutive runs of alphabetical letter-pairs in a common word (mn, de, st).

deeded = The most common word consisting of two different letters each of which is used three times.

defenselessness = The longest common word with one vowel only (repeated).

deinstitutionalized = The longest word beginning and ending with the letter *D*.

discreet, discrete = The longest homophonic anagrams, words with the same pronunciation and with the same letters (differently arranged) but with different spellings and meanings.

draughtboards = The longest two-syllable word beginning with the letter *D* (checkerboards).

draughts = The longest one-syllable word beginning with the letter *D*.

Earth, Mars = The only planet names with anagrams, *Earth* yields *hater* and *heart*, and *Mars* yields *arms* and *rams*.

earthed = The longest one-syllable word beginning with the letter *E*.

earthtongues = The longest two-syllable word beginning with the letter *E*, it is the pluralized name of a fungus.

eensie-weensie = The longest hyphenated word consisting of two identical parts except for the middle letter.

eleven = The longest number word with alternating vowels and consonants.

encourage = The longest common word in which changing one letter radically changes its pronunciation (*encourage → entourage*).

epizootiological = The shortest nine-syllable word; the

word is the adjectival form of *epizootiology*, the study of the occurrence and spread of animal diseases.

epizootiologically = The shortest ten-syllable word.

epizootiology = The shortest eight-syllable word.

Euboia, eunoia, Euodia = The shortest words with all five regular vowels. *Euboia*, one of the few spellings of the name of the largest island in the Aegean Sea, is a proper noun. *Euodia* is the name of a Christian woman who, according to the New Testament, quarreled with Syntyche. *Eunoia* describes a normal or healthy mental state.

first, forty = The only number words whose letters appear in alphabetical order.

flameproof = The longest word beginning and ending with the letter *F.*

flameproofed = The longest two-syllable word beginning with the letter *F.*

flinched = The longest one-syllable word beginning with the letter *F.*

four = The only number word whose quantity of letters matches the number it denotes.

grouched = The longest one-syllable word beginning with the letter *G.*

groundsheets = The longest two-syllable word beginning with the letter *G*, it describes waterproof sheets placed on the ground for protection (as of a sleeping bag) against moisture.

gyp, gyppy = The only English words that consist entirely of lowercase letters that go below the body (descenders). The expression *gyppy tummy* describes diarrhea contracted especially by travelers.

hairsbreadth = The longest two-syllable word beginning with the letter *H.*

haunched = The longest one-syllable word beginning with the letter *H*.

hazardous, horrendous, stupendous, tremendous = The only four common words ending in *-dous*. Others include *apodous* (footless), *iodous* (relating to or containing iodine), *macropodous* (of plants, having a long stem or stalk), *molybdous* (of, relating to, or containing molybdenum), and *vanadous* (of, relating to, or containing vanadium).

hereof, of, thereof, whereof = The only words in which the letter *F* is pronounced like a *V*.

HOMOTAXIA = Possibly the longest word composed entirely of letters with vertical symmetry in uppercase, *homotaxia* describes similarity in fossil content and in order of arrangement of stratified deposits.

honorificabilitudinitatibus = The longest word consisting of alternating consonants and vowels, it means "the state of being able to achieve honors" and appears in Shakespeare's *Love's Labour's Lost*. Other long words with alternating consonants and vowels are *aluminosilicates*, *parasitological*, *verisimilitudes*, and *supererogatorily*.

hydroxyzine = The only word (besides its plural) containing the letters *XYZ*, *hydroxyzine* describes a tranquilizer and antihistamine that is an ether alcohol.

inadequacies = The longest common word containing five consonants.

inoperative = The word with the most letters from the second part of the alphabet (*M–Z*); six out of its eleven letters are from the second part of the alphabet.

interrogatives, reinvestigator, tergiversation = The

largest three nonscientific words that are anagrams of one another.

inthralled = The longest two-syllable word beginning with the letter *I*; it means "enthralled."

itched = The longest one-syllable word beginning with the letter *I*.

James Madison = The only U.S. president whose first and last names alternate between consonants and vowels.

jinni = The word, another spelling of *genie*, becomes plural not by adding any letter but by removing the last letter: *jinn*.

johnny-jump-up, niminy-piminy = The longest words that would normally be typed with only the right hand using standard keyboarding. *Niminy-piminy* means "ridiculously delicate," and *johnny-jump-up* is the common name of the wild pansy.

jounced = The longest one-syllable word beginning with the letter *J*; it is past tense of *jounce* (to fall, drop, or bounce so as to shake).

Juneteenths = The longest one-syllable word beginning with the letter *J*. *Juneteenths* is the plural of the name of a Texas holiday celebrated on June 19 honoring the emancipation of slaves in the state.

Kauaiian = A geographical adjective containing six consecutive vowels; an uncommon variant of *Kauaian*.

kayak = The longest common palindrome beginning with the letter *K*.

kine = The archaic plural of *cow* shares none of its letters.

knickknacks = The longest two-syllable word beginning with the letter *K*.

Lake Mijijie = A lake in Australia with five consecutive dotted letters when written in lowercase.

launched = The longest one-syllable word beginning with the letter *L*.

lawn tennis court = Among the longest expressions with the five regular vowels in alphabetical order.

lighttight, lillypilly = The longest words consisting only of ascending letters (b, d, f, h, k, t), descending letters (g, j, p, q, y), or dots (i, j) in lowercase. *Lighttight* means "lightproof," and *lillypilly* names an Australian tree with hard fine-grained wood.

llama = The only common English word beginning with a double consonant. (The proper name *Llewellyn* isn't as common.)

March, April, May = The only months with anagrammatical names. *March* yields *charm*; *April* yields *ripal*, which, can be a first name when capitalized and which, in lowercase, is a synonym for *riparian* (of, relating to, or situated on, a riverbank). *May* yields *yam*.

meet-her-in-the-entry-kiss-her-in-the-buttery = Besides being the longest nontechnical plant name, the entry is one of the few English words with nine hyphens.

moosetongues = The longest two-syllable word beginning with the letter *M*; it describes willow herbs.

Muammar Khadafi = The late Libyan leader had a name with up to 112 variants: 72, according to the U.S. Library of Congress and 40 additional spellings have been used by the *New York Times* and Associated Press. Here are the 112:

Al-Gathafi, Muammar
al-Qadhafi, Muammar

Al Qathafi, Mu'ammar
Al Qathafi, Muammar
El Gaddafi, Moamar
El Kadhafi, Moammar
El Kazzafi, Moamer
El Qathafi, Mu'Ammar
Gadafi, Muammar
Gaddafi, Moamar
Gadhafi, Mo'ammar
Gathafi, Muammar
Ghadafi, Muammar
Ghaddafi, Muammar
Ghaddafy, Muammar
Gheddafi, Muammar
Gheddafi, Muhammar
Kadaffi, Momar
Kad'afi, Mu`amar
Kaddafi, Muamar
Kaddafi, Muammar
Kadhafi, Moammar
Kadhafi, Mouammar
Kazzafi, Moammar
Khadafy, Moammar
Khaddafi, Muammar
Moamar al-Gaddafi
Moamar el Gaddafi
Moamar El Kadhafi
Moamar Gaddafi
Moamer El Kazzafi
Mo'ammar el-Gadhafi
Moammar El Kadhafi
Mo'ammar Gadhafi
Moammar Kadhafi
Moammar Khadafy

Moammar Qudhafi
Mu`amar al-Kad'afi
Mu'amar al-Kadafi
Muamar Al-Kaddafi
Muamar Kaddafi
Muamer Gadafi
Muammar Al-Gathafi
Muammar al-Khaddafi
Mu'ammar al-Qadafi
Mu'ammar al-Qaddafi
Muammar al-Qadhafi
Mu'ammar al-Qadhdhafi
Mu`ammar al-Qadhdhāfī
Mu'ammar Al Qathafi
Muammar Al Qathafi
Muammar Gadafi
Muammar Gaddafi
Muammar Ghadafi
Muammar Ghaddafi
Muammar Ghaddafy
Muammar Gheddafi
Muammar Kaddafi
Muammar Khaddafi
Mu'ammar Qadafi
Muammar Qaddafi
Muammar Qadhafi
Mu'ammar Qadhdhafi
Muammar Quathafi
Mulazim Awwal Mu'ammar Muhammad Abu Min-
    yar al-Qadhafi
Qadafi, Mu'ammar
Qaddafi, Muammar
Qadhafi, Muammar
Qadhdhāfī, Mu`ammar

Qathafi, Mu'Ammar
Quathafi, Muammar
Qudhafi, Moammar
Moamar AI Kadafi
Maummar Gaddafi
Moamar Gadhafi
Moamer Gaddafi
Moamer Kadhafi
Moamma Gaddafi
Moammar Gaddafi
Moammar Gadhafi
Moammar Ghadafi
Moammar Khadaffy
Moammar Khaddafi
Moammar el Gadhafi
Moammer Gaddafi
Mouammer al Gaddafi
Muamar Gaddafi
Muammar Al Ghaddafi
Muammar Al Qaddafi
Muammar Al Qaddafi
Muammar El Qaddafi
Muammar Gadaffi
Muammar Gadafy
Muammar Gaddhafi
Muammar Gadhafi
Muammar Ghadaffi
Muammar Qadthafi
Muammar al Gaddafi
Muammar el Gaddafy
Muammar el Gaddafi
Muammar el Qaddafi
Muammer Gadaffi
Muammer Gaddafi

Mummar Gaddafi
Omar Al Qathafi
Omar Mouammer Al Gaddafi
Omar Muammar Al Ghaddafi
Omar Muammar Al Qaddafi
Omar Muammar Al Qathafi
Omar Muammar Gaddafi
Omar Muammar Ghaddafi
Omar al Ghaddafi

multiculturalism = The longest common word beginning and ending with the letter *M*.

murmur = The longest common word beginning with the letter *M* consisting of two identical syllables (tautonym).

Muroidea = Possibly the shortest word with all five regular vowels in reverse alphabetical order. *Muroidea* describes a superfamily of rodents that includes hamsters, gerbils, true mice, and rats. Longer words with that property include *duoliteral*, *subcontinental*, *uncomplimentary*, and *unoriental*.

naughts = The longest one-syllable word beginning with the letter *N*.

nightclothes = The longest two-syllable word beginning with the letter *N*.

nonsupports, nontortuous = Prime examples of two of the longest words made up of only letters from the second half of the alphabet.

nonunion = The longest word containing the letter *N* as the only consonant.

Oceania = The collective name for about 25,000 Pacific islands has seven letters yet five syllables.

oinked = The longest one-syllable word beginning with the letter *O*.

one = The only number word in reverse alphabetical order.

Ouenouaou = The name of a stream in the Philippines, the word is the longest known place name with only one consonant.

ough-, -ough, -ough- = The combination *ough* can be pronounced in nine different ways:

A rough-coated, dough-faced, thoughtful plough-man strode through the streets of Scarborough; after falling into a slough, he coughed and hic-coughed.

outstretched = The longest two-syllable word beginning with the letter *O*.

overnumerousnesses = The longest word with no ascending letters, no descending letters, or dots in lowercase. The word is a bit artificial but is longer than its competitors, including *curvaceousnesses* and *overnumerousness*.

ploughwrights = The longest two-syllable word beginning with the letter *P*.

preached = The longest one-syllable word beginning with the letter *P*.

quenched = The longest one-syllable word beginning with the letter *Q*.

queue = The only word pronounced the same after losing its last four letters (see *aitch*).

queuing = The only common word with five vowels in a row. *Mioued* and *miaouing* are unusual spellings of the more usual *meowed* and *meowing*. *Cooeeing*, which describes a peculiar cry by the Australian aborigines, is uncommon.

reached = The longest one-syllable word beginning with the letter *R*.

redivider = The longest common palindromic word.

restaurateur = The longest common word beginning and ending with the letter *R*.

restaurateurs = The longest balanced word, a word in which a central letter, acting as a fulcrum, separates and "balances" the same set of letters (though possibly differently arranged). In this case, the *R* is between the letters *A*, *E*, *R*, *S*, *T*, and *U*.

rhythms = The longest common word without any of the regular five vowels, *rhythms* has two syllables but only one vowel.

roughstrings = The longest two-syllable word beginning with the letter *R*, it describes pieces of undressed timber put under the steps of a wooden stair for their support.

rupturewort = The longest word that can be typed using only the top row of a QWERTY keyboard, *rupturewort* names an Old World herb. Curiously, *typewriter* is also one of the longest words that can be typed on the top row.

scratchbrushed = The longest two-syllable word beginning with the letter *S*, it describes something brushed with a stiff wire brush for cleaning metal.

sequoia, miaoued, dialogue, equation = *Sequoia* and *miaoued* are the most common seven-letter words with each of the five regular vowels appearing only once. *Dialogue* and *equation* are the most common eight-letter words similarly rich in vowels. There are some other words with the same property, but they are esoteric. *Eulogia* describes bread that is blessed but not consecrated and that is consumed after religious services by worshipers who didn't participate in communion. *Eunomia* means "eunomy" (civil order under good laws).

sestettes = A word each of whose letters occurs exactly three times.

Shakalshas = The longest word that can be typed using only the middle row of a QWERTY keyboard, *Shakalshas* describes a people emigrating from Phrygia and colonizing Sicily in early times. The middle row can also yield *Hadassah* (the name of the benevolent organization of Jewish women) and *haggadah* (the name of the book of readings for the Passover Seder service).

sponged, wronged = The longest words in reverse alphabetical order, with no letters repeated.

spoonfeed = The longest word with letters in reverse alphabetical order, with some letters repeated.

squirreled = The longest common word often pronounced as only one syllable, though it is often pronounced disyllabically in England. Other long monosyllabic words are *scratched, screeched, scrounged, straights, strengths,* and *squelched.*

strengthlessnesses = The longest word with only one vowel (repeated) that isn't a proper noun. It would be difficult to use the word because it pluralizes an abstract quality. If we resorted to proper nouns, *Chrononhotonthologos,* a satirical eighteenth-century play by English poet and songwriter Henry Carey, may be the longest English word with only one vowel (repeated).

strengths = The longest word with exactly one vowel (nonrepeated).

stressed, desserts = The longest common semordnilaps, words that spell other words when spelled backward.

sulphonphthaleins = The pluralized chemical term is possibly the longest word containing all five regular vowels only once and no letter *Y*.

superstuffed, overstuffed, understudy, superstud = Some of the few words with four adjacent letters of the alphabet in order (rstu).

syzygy = The only current (though esoteric) English word with three *Y*s, *syzygy* describes the conjunction or opposition of any two heavenly bodies (see *twyndyllyngs*).

ten = The only number word that spells another word when it is spelled backward (semordnilap).

testes = The longest common word beginning with the letter *T* that is composed of two identical syllables (tautonym).

therein = A word containing ten words with letters adjacent and in order: *ere*, *her*, *herein*, *re*, *the*, *he*, *here*, *in*, *rein*, and *there*.

thoughts = The longest one-syllable word beginning with the letter *T*.

throatstraps = The longest two-syllable word beginning with the letter *T*, the word describes bridles or halters passing under horses' throats.

tmesis = The only word beginning with *tm*-, *tmesis* describes separating the parts of a compound word by one or more words, as in *what price so ever* for *whatsoever price*.

transubstantiationalist = The longest uncommon word beginning and ending with the letter *T*, it describes a believer in the actual presence of Christ in the bread and wine of the Eucharist.

twyndyllyngs = The plural of an old word for a twin or twinling; it is the longest word without any of the five regular vowels.

uncomplimentary, unnoticeably, subcontinental = The most common words with vowels in reverse alphabetical order. A few other words with that property exist, such as *quodlibetary*, the adjectival form of *quodlibet*, which can describe a few things, especially a subtle or debatable point within a scholastic or theological debate. There is also *duoliteral*, which is in Webster's 1913 dictionary and which means "consisting of two letters only." *Muscoidea* describes a superfamily of insects to which the common housefly belongs.

uncopyrightable = The longest common word with no letter of the alphabet occurring more than once (the definition of an isogram). *Ambidextrously* is a close second. *Subdermatoglyphic*, which means "pertaining to the layers of skin beneath the fingertips," is often listed as the longest isogram in English.

United Arab Emirates = The longest name of a country consisting of alternating vowels and consonants.

unnoticeably = The shortest word with the five major vowels and *Y* in reverse alphabetical order, each occurring exactly once.

unprosperousness = The longest word each of whose letters occurs exactly twice.

ushers = The only English word with five personal pronouns in succession—namely, *us*, *she*, *he*, *her*, and *hers*.

versesmiths = The longest two-syllable word beginning with the letter *V*, it describes writers of light or poor verse.

vouched = The longest one-syllable word beginning with the letter *V*.

widow = The only female form in English that is shorter than the corresponding male term (widower).

wreathed = The longest one-syllable word beginning with the letter *W*.

xysts = The longest one-syllable word beginning with the letter *X*, it describes either long and open porticoes or tree-lined walkways.

yearned = The longest one-syllable word beginning with the letter *Y*.

yesterday = The longest common word beginning and ending with the letter *Y*.

yourselves = The longest two-syllable word beginning with the letter *Y*.

zeitgeists = The longest two-syllable word beginning with the letter *Z*, it describes spirits of the times.

Zouaves = The longest one-syllable word beginning with the letter *Z*, it describes members of French infantry who were Algerians.

Funny or Outlandish Homophonic Names in Real Phone and Address Directories

Every one of the names that are listed sectioning this appendix is available on Zabasearch.com and is officially linked to a phone number and usually a mailing address. Many of the names were seriously given to people by parents who didn't realize how many people have dirty minds. My apologies to Sharon Siemen, whose name can be treated as a double pun. Many last names aren't funny until one adds certain first names. Again, my apologies to Sharon Siemen. Some names aren't funny in the language of origin, such as "Phat," though I'm suspicious of "Phat Clod," the name of a resident of Lowell, Massachusetts.

Other names were created as puns that work because of a combination of words. A few years ago someone interviewed a homeowner in California whose house was threatened but ultimately not touched by a fire. The interviewee, who appeared to be quite serious, gave his name as "Mike Litoris," which sounds suspiciously like "my clitoris." The name seems about as honest as the figures for our federal budget. One wag who was commenting over the Internet on the interview with "Mike Litoris" said that it was a great achievement by interviewer "Dixie Normous," a name that sounds suspiciously like "dick's enormous." An irony is that, although both names appear to be equally phony, we can at least reach "Dixie Normous," who, according to Zabasearch.com, has an appropriate address—one in Washington, DC.

Some names are funny not because they are ridiculously self-depreciating (such as "Phat Clod"), or because they are ridiculously boastful (such as "Dixie Normous"), but because they are insulting to others. Just ask "Kiss Myass" from Ossining, New York.

Many first and last names that are funny in combination were not, however, intended to be funny. For example, many of us know people with the surname "Easter." Many males with that surname are named Michael. Further, many Michaels become Mikes. Although the name "Michael" isn't funny, and "Mike" isn't funny, something magical happens when "Mike" immediately precedes "Easter." The result is "Mike Easter," which sounds like "my keister," which, in slang, can mean "my buttocks."

Although the word *turd* is funny to many people, the name "Etta M. Turd" isn't on the list, though it's listed on Zabasearch.com. "Dennis Turd" wasn't even in the running, though "Etta A. Turd" or even "Etta Turd" would have made the list had I found those names. Unfortunately, there were only two Turds on Zabasearch.com, and Etta M. is from Idaho, one of the least funny states.

I readily admit that many but by no means all listed names are gag names. Many others are just accidental homophones, which just happen to sound like other words. As to the gag names, the name "Alotta Fagina" quickly comes to mind. Its best-known bearer was a villain (or villainess, if one prefers) in *Austin Powers: International Man of Mystery.* "Ivana Humpalot" is the name of a voluptuous Russian woman in *Austin Powers: The Spy Who Shagged Me.* One Austin Powers character who came close to making it on the list was Fook Yu, the twin of Fook Mi in *Austin Powers in Goldmember.* Someone named "Fook M. Yu" (close but no cigar) is supposed to live in Michigan, according to Zabasearch.com.

Gag names can become well known because of not only movies but also TV shows. *The Simpsons* TV show included prank phone calls from Bart Simpson to Moe's Tavern in which Bart asked Moe Syzlak to page several names on my list, including "Mike Rotch," "Seymour Butts," "Amanda Huggenkiss," and "Hugh Jass." In the mid-1970s two young men named Jim Davidson and John Elmo often called the Tube Bar in Jersey City and asked for patrons with such names as "Ben Dover," "Holden McGroin," and "Al Coholic." It is said that those prank calls, which were recorded, inspired the names used in Bart Simpson's prank calls to Moe's Tavern. I can't determine for sure the source or sources of those names, but I do know that most of the names mentioned on *The Simpsons* are on my list.

400-PLUS OUTLANDISH NAMES

Every name here is listed in Zabasearch.com. By each name I've listed a city of residence where the name's user either lives or has lived.

A. Blinkin (Colma, California)

A. C. Current (Gastonia, North Carolina)

Adam Baum (Canoga Park, California)

Ailieen Too (Dana Point, California)

Al Bino (Sinking Spring, Pennsylvania)

Al Cahall (Albuquerque, New Mexico)

Al Coholic (Madison, Alabama)

Al Dente (New York, New York)

Al Fresco (Tucson, Arizona)

Alison Wonderland (Cambridge, Massachusetts)

Al K. Seltzer (Chicago, Illinois)

Allie Katt (Boulder, Colorado)

Al L. Vera (Mt. Holly, New Jersey)

Alotta Fagina (Denver, Colorado)

Amanda Hugankiss (Dover, New Hampshire)

Amanda Hugenkiss (Leawood, Kansas)

Amelia Cook (Scottsdale, Arizona)

Amos B. Haven (San Francisco, California)

A. Ness (Denver, Colorado)

Angie Gram (Chesterton, Indiana)

Anita Bath (Portland, Maine)

Anita Beaver (Noblesville, Indiana)

Anita Beer (Hollister, Missouri)

Anita Bohn (Marco, Florida)

Anita Book (Ormond Beach, Florida)

Anita Break (Bakersfield, California)

Anita Carr (Grand Bay, Alabama)

Anita Dick (Birmingham, Alabama)

Anita Doctor (Fitzgerald, Georgia)

Anita Gay (Los Angeles, California)

Anita Guy (Stone Mountain, Georgia)

Anita Hammer (Augusta, Georgia)

Anita Hand (Birmingham, Alabama)

Anita Hoare (Cleveland, Ohio)

Anita Hug (Albany, New York)
Anita Job (Redlands, California)
Anita Jump (Fort Thomas, Kentucky)
Anita Knapp (Bay City, Texas)
Anita Kopp (North Mankato, Minnesota)
Anita Lay (Fernandina Beach, Florida)
Anita Little (Montgomery, Alabama)
Anita Lott (Mobile, Alabama)
Anita Mann (Cullman, Alabama)
Anita Nail (Columbus, Ohio)
Anita Nurse (Dorchester, Massachusetts)
Anita Plummer (Connersville, Indiana)
Anita Raisor (Louisville, Kentucky)
Anita Shake (Fairborn, Georgia)
Anita Sipp (Mobile, Alabama)
Anna Graham (Burbank, California)
Anna Prentice (Hot Springs, Arkansas)
Anna Rexia (Austin, Texas)
Anna Sasin (Happy Valley, Oregon)
April Schauer (Winnetka, California)
April Showers (Hot Springs, Arkansas)
Armand Hammer (Falls Church, Virginia)
Art Major (Apache Junction, Arizona)
Art Sellers (Red Oak, Iowa))
A. Satan (Oklahoma City, Oklahoma)
Barbara Seville (San Juan Capistrano, California)
Barb Dwyer (Seattle, Washington)
Barbie Dahl (Daly City, California)
Barry Cade (Poughkeepsie, New York)
Barry Tone (Reno, Nevada)
B. A. Ware (Loma Linda, California)
B. Cheesy (Gainesville, Texas)
Bea Minor (Leander, Texas)
Ben Dover (Alexander City, Alabama)

Ben Down (Redonda Beach, California)

Ben Gay (Suffield, Connecticut)

Ben Lyon (Dothan, Alabama)

Ben Thair (Clearwater, Florida)

Bertha D. Blues (Philadelphia, Pennsylvania)

Betty B. Ready (Springfield, Missouri)

Betty Bye (Marysville, California)

Bich C. Ho (Winnetka, California)

Bill Board (Akron, Ohio)

Bill Ding (New York, New York)

Billy Stick (Waite Park, Minnesota)

Blonde Too (Claremont, California)

B. Mum (Lockport, New York)

Bob Katz (Champaign, Illinois)

Bob Wire (Hollywood, Florida)

Brad Hammer (Washington, DC)

Brock Lee (Fresno, California)

Brooke Trout (Castle Rock, Colorado)

B. Sting (Valparaiso, Indiana)

Bud Light (Chelsea, Alabama)

Bud Weiser (Sarasota, Florida)

Bul Dung (Worcester, Massachusetts)

Buster Cherry (Miramar, Florida)

Buster Hyman (Birmingham, Alabama)

Buster Load (Elkins Park, Pennsylvania)

Cam Payne (Salem, Indiana)

Candy Barr (Denver, Colorado)

Candy Cain (Navarre, Florida)

Cara Van (Burton, Texas)

Charity Case (Georgetown Township, Michigan)

Cheri Pitts (Warren, Ohio)

Chris Coe (Kimberly, Idaho)

Chris Cross (San Pedro, California)

Chris P. Bacon (Elizabeth, Louisiana)

Chu A. Wang (Fullerton, California)

Chuck Wagon (Corona, California)

Claire Voyant (Titusville, Florida)

Clara Net (Selma, Arizona)

Coal Slaw (Piscataway, New Jersey)

Cole Kutz (Mansfield, Missouri)

Colin Sick (Rochester, New York)

Cookie Cream (Dallas, Texas)

Corey A. Graff (Topton, Pennsylvania)

Cori Ander (Minneapolis, Minnesota)

Craven Moorehead (Jacksonville, Florida)

Crusty Flake (Minot, North Dakota)

Crystal Ball (Fort Mitchell, Alabama)

Crystal Glass (Bradley, Arkansas)

Crystal Water (Coldwater, Mississippi)

C. Senor (Chicago, Illinois)

C. Titts (Gastonia, North Carolina)

Curl N. Rod (Chicago, Illinois)

Curtis E. Counts (Schlater, Mississippi)

C. Worthy (Auburn, Alabama)

Dan D. Lyons (Carbondale, Colorado)

Dan Druff (Kingwood, Texas)

Darren Deeds (Huntington, West Virginia)

Dawn Schauers (Pottsville, Pennsylvania)

Dee Flower (Nashville, Tennessee)

Dee Major (Pembroke Pines, Florida)

D. Generate (St. Petersburg, Florida)

Dialed Also (Baton Rouge, Louisiana)

Dick Boner (Oceanside, California)

Dick Burns (Soquel, California)

Dick Fitzwell (Appleton, Wisconsin)

Dick Groh (Novato, California)

Dick Hard (Yankton, South Dakota)

Dick Head (Sandy, Utah)

Dick Hertz (Polson, Montana)

Dick Hood (Oklahoma City, Oklahoma)

Dick Hunter (Mesa, Arizona)

Dick Long (Heber, Arizona)

Dick Short (Montgomery, Alabama)

Dick Wood (The Village, Florida)

Dill Doe (Fort Worth, Texas)

Dina Soares (Providence, Rhode Island)

Dixie Normous (Washington, DC)

Dixon Butt (Frederick, Maryland)

Dixon Ho (San Jose, California)

Donald Duck (Alexander City, Alabama)

Donna C. Rat (Blountsville, Alabama)

Donny Brook (Grove City, Ohio)

Doris Schutt (Portland, Texas)

Doug Graves (Beebe, Arkansas)

Doug Hole (Rockford, Ohio)

Douglas Fur (Bloomfield, Iowa))

Drew A. Blanc (Schaumburg, Illinois)

Dusty Rhodes (Alvin, Texas)

Earl E. Bird (Goreville, Illinois)

Earl E. Riser (Butler, Indiana)

Easton West (New Paris, Indiana)

Eden Cherry (Powder Spring, Georgia)

E. Goh (Torrance, California)

Eileen Dover (San Francisco, California)

Ella Vader (Denver, Colorado)

E. Nuff (Virginia Beach, Virginia)

Eric Shinn (Hudson, Florida)

Ernest Juri (Clearlake, California)

Ewe Goh (Hyattsville, Maryland)

Forrest Green (Mesa, Arizona)

Frank N. Stein (Milford, Delaware)

Gail Storm (Bellingham, Virginia)

Gary C. Crotch (Methuen, Massachusetts)
Gaye Hooker (San Angelo, Texas)
Gene Poole (Northport, Alabama)
Ginger Snap (Riverside, California)
Ginger Snaps (Manhattan, Montana)
Graham Cracker (Austin, Texas)
Harry Balls (Sanford, Florida)
Harry Beaver (Roy, Washington)
Harry Bush (Ashland, Kentucky)
Harry Dicks (Boca Raton, Florida)
Harry Kuntz (Dickinson, North Dakota)
Haywood Jablowme (Mishawaka, Indiana)
Hazel Nutt (Chataignier, Louisiana)
Heaven Coming (Carmel, California)
Hedda Lettuce (Elkhart, Indiana)
Helen Back (Fort Walton Beach, Florida)
Harry Pitts (Berlin, Maryland)
Holden McGroin (St. Petersburg, Florida)
Holdin Chestnut (Bronx, New York)
Holdin Donkey (Yonkers, New York)
Holdin Peace (Forest City, North Carolina)
Holdin Shanique (Fayetteville, North Carolina)
Holdin Spyglass (Houston, Texas)
Holly Day (Lawndale, California)
House Crack (Columbus, Ohio)
Hugh A. Glasscock (Lebanon, Kentucky)
Hugh G. Rection (Greensboro, North Carolina)
Hugh Jass (San Jose, Arkansas)
Hugh Mungus (Steamboat Springs, Colorado)
Hung Lo (Los Angeles, California)
I. A. Cumming (Lakeland, Florida)
I. A. Going (Springfield, Illinois)
I. B. Bee (Beverly Hills, Florida)
Ice C. That (Adrian, Michigan)

Ida Clair (Pocahontas, Arkansas)
Ida Eaton (Hephzibah, Georgia)
Ida Felt (Staten Island, New York)
Ida Lain (Kansas City, Missouri)
I. F. You (Dallas, Texas)
I. Loser (Youngstown, Ohio)
Ima Johnson (Elkins, Arkansas)
Ima Klutz (Lakeville, Minnesota)
Ima Winner (Barrington, Illinois)
I. M. Cheesy (Austin, Texas)
In Ass (Dover Foxcroft, Maine)
Iona Carr (Blue Springs, Missouri)
I. P. Daily (York, Pennsylvania)
I. P. Freely (Mechanicsburg, Pennsylvania)
Ivana Humpalot (Boone, North Carolina)
Ivana Tinkle (Atlanta, Georgia)
Jack Ass (Tucson, Arizona)
Jack Cass (Crete, Illinois)
Jack Kass (Gretna, Louisiana)
Jack Mehoff (Belmont, California)
Jack Off (Dyersburg, Tennessee)
Jacques Strap (San Marcos, Texas)
Jed Dye (Swainsboro, Georgia)
Jerry Rigg (Apache Junction, Arizona)
Jess Tate (Hoxie, Arkansas)
Jim Nasium (Atlanta, Georgia)
Jim Shortz (Winter Park, Florida)
Jim Shu (Pompano Beach, Florida)
Jim Sox (Bacliff, Texas)
Jordan Rivers (Eau Claire, Wisconsin)
Joy Rider (Hinleah, Florida)
June Bugg (Pensacola, Florida)
Justin Case (Florence, Alabama)
Justin Credible (Rockland, Maine)

Justin Hale (Grand Bay, Alabama)
Justin Tyme (West Hills, California)
Kandi Apple (Russells Point, Ohio)
Kandi Kane (Altavista, Virginia)
Ken Dahl (Sedona, Arizona)
Kiss Myass (Ossining, New York)
Kitty Cat (Gardendale, Alabama)
Kitty Katz (Lake Worth, Florida)
Lance A. Boyle (Hyattsville, Maryland)
Latoya Stinx (Greensboro, North Carolina)
Laura Lynn Hardy (Birmingham, Alabama)
Let Shit (Omaha, Nebraska)
Lewis N. Clark (Ellensburg, Washington)
Lisa House (Big Bear City, California)
Lon Moore (Birmingham, Alabama)
Lynn C. Doyle (Mobile, Alabama)
Major Payne (Blairsville, Georgia)
Mark Mysac (St. Augustine, Florida)
Marshall Law (Birmingham, Alabama)
Marty Graw (Dayton, Ohio)
Mary A. Richman (Lynchburg, Tennessee)
Mary Christmas (Americus, Georgia)
Mary Gold (Alameda, California)
Mary Juana (Los Angeles, California)
Mary Me (Ames, Iowa)
Mary Money (Hesperia, California)
Max E. Pad (Bloomingdale, Illinois)
Max Load (Phoenixville, Pennsylvania)
M. Baumer (Bay City, Michigan)
Megan M. Bacon (Grand Rapids, Michigan)
Melba Crisp (Bonne Terre, Maryland)
Melba Toast (Jackson, Mississippi)
Melody Music (Tampa, Florida)
Mercedes Benz (Jacksonville, Florida)

Michael A. Bearcomesout (Billings, Montana)
Michael Pukes (Cumberland, Wisconsin)
Mike Easter (Hoover, Alabama)
Mike Hock (Walnut Creek, California)
Mike Hunt (Encinitas, California)
Mike Oxbig (St. Louis, Missouri)
Mike Raffone (Boynton Beach, Florida)
Mike Rotch (Jackson, Alabama)
Misty Waters (Frierson, Louisiana)
Moe Lester (Cullowhee, North Carolina)
Molly Kuehl (Catonsville, Maryland)
Mona Little (Sabetha, Kansas)
Mona Lott (Miami, Florida)
Monica Monica (Phoenix, Arizona)
M. T. Head (Greenwood, Mississippi)
Much S. So (Chicago, Illinois)
Much Too (Pleasant Hill, California)
Much Y. So (Seattle, Washington)
Munch Dick (L'Anse, Michigan)
Munch S. Whitten (Hobe Sound, Florida)
Myles Long (Metairie, Louisiana)
Myles Short (Salida, Colorado)
Myra Mains (Saint George, Utah)
N. E. Howe (Lake Wales, Florida)
Noah Ark (Port Hueneme, California)
Noah Flood (Park City, Utah)
Noah Lott (Niles, Ohio)
Noah Peel (Pine Bluff, Arkansas)
Noah Riddle (Merrill, Wisconsin)
Noahs Ark (Orlando, Florida)
Noah Zark (Finksburg, Maryland)
N. Thyme (Chicago, Illinois)
On D. Dick (Pekin, Illinois)
Ophelia Cox (Knoxville, Tennessee)

Ophelia Payne (Olive Branch, Mississippi)
Otto Glass (Rosebud, Texas)
Otto Graf (Millbrae, California)
Paige Turner (Florence, Alabama)
Park A. Studebaker (Dayton, Ohio)
Parker Carr (Pasco, Washington)
Patrick Drips (Elkader, Iowa))
Paul Bearer (Mechanicsville, Maryland)
P. Brain (Greensburg, Pennsylvania)
P. Cock (Santa Barbara, California)
Pearl E. Gates (Gilbert, Arizona)
Pearly Gates (Midlothian, Virginia)
Penny Lane (Goshen, Kentucky)
Penny Loafer (Austin, Texas)
Penny Wise (Turlock, California)
Peter Abbott (St. Petersburg, Florida)
Peter Stiff (Santa Monica, California)
Phat Clod (Lowell, Massachusetts)
Phil Beaver (Frenchlick, Indiana)
Phil McCracken (Bakersville, California)
P. Hole (Flagstaff, Arizona)
P. Ness (Gerlach, Nevada)
P. Nutt (El Cajun, California)
Price Wright (Duarte, California)
Pteryl Dactyl (Albion, California)
Randy Lover (Goffstown, New Hampshire)
Randy Pigg (North Little Rock, Arkansas)
Ray Gunn (Burnsville, Minnesota)
Rays D. Devil (Tampa, Florida)
Reignhbeau Leeves (Milwaukee, Wisconsin)
Rich Guy (New Port Richey, Florida)
Rich Jerk (Yuba City, California)
Rick O'Shea (East Sound, Washington)
Rick Shaw (Anderson, Indiana)

Rita Booke (Fort Collins, Colorado)

R. M. Pitt (Louisville, Kentucky)

Robin Banks (Little Rock, Arkansas)

Robin Money (Hernando, Florida)

Rocky Roads (Brighton, Colorado)

Rose Bush (Centre, Alabama)

Rufus Leaking (Houston, Texas)

Russ D. Carr (Brighton, Colorado)

Rusty Hinge (Crane, Missouri)

Rusty Pipes (Bossier City, California)

Rusty Steele (Colorado Springs, Colorado)

Sal Minella (San Ramon, California)

Sandra Sux (Houston, Texas)

Sandy Shore (Big Bear Lake, California)

Sarah Bellum (Denver, Colorado)

Sara Tonin (Youngwood, Pennsylvania)

Scott Free (Phoenix, Arizona)

Seymour Butts (Jacksonville, Florida)

Sharon A. Butt (Titusville, New Jersey)

Sharon A. Bone (Tamarac, Florida)

Sharon A. Woody (Butte, Montana)

Sharon B. Hind (Apache Junction, Arizona)

Sharon Butts (Lithonia, Georgia)

Sharon E. Boys (Shakopee, Minnesota)

Sharon Needles (St. Joseph, Illinois)

Sharon R. Cooter (Arvada, Colorado)

Sharon Siemen (Georgetown Township, Michigan)

Sharon Weed (Indio, California)

Sheila Blige (Brunswick, Georgia)

Sherman Tank (Lodgepole, Nebraska)

Snow White (Jonesboro, Georgia)

Sonny Day (Portland, Maine)

Stanley Cupp (Cumberland, Wisconsin)

Sterling Silva (North Hollywood, California)

Stu Pid (New Mexico)
Summer Day (Santa Cruz, California)
Sur Fat Rat (National City, California)
Swe T. Too (Arcadia, California)
Tad Moore (Opp, Alabama)
Tanya Hyde (Rialto, California)
Teddy Baer (Fort Lauderdale, Florida)
Ted E. Baer (Palo Alto, California)
Teresa Green (Bridgeport, Connecticut)
Terryl G. Dactyl (Los Gatos, California)
Teresa Green (Bridgeport, Connecticut)
Throw Stones (Tekonsha, Michigan)
Tim Burr (Harrison, Arkansas)
Tish Hughes (Lakeland, Florida)
Tom Katz (Bentonville, Arkansas)
Tommy Gunn (Alexander City, Alabama)
Victor E. March (Phoenix, Arizona)
Virginia Beach (Park Hill, Oklahoma)
Walker Kidd (Prestonsburg, Kentucky)
Warren Peace (Glendale, Arizona)
Wendy Dewer (Fayetteville, Arkansas)
Wendy Show (Buckeye, Arizona)
Winsome Ho (Pittsburgh, Pennsylvania)
Winsom Harley (Palm Bay, Florida)
Winsom Iras (Nantucket, Massachusetts)
X. Crack (Auburn, Maine)
X. Satan (San Antonio, Texas)
Zhengang Zong (Plainsboro, New Jersey)

SELECTED BIBLIOGRAPHY

Agee, Jon. *Go Hang a Salami! I'm a Lasagna Hog!: And Other Palindromes.* New York: Farrar, Straus & Giroux, 1994.

——. *Palindromania!* New York: Farrar, Straus & Giroux, 2009.

Ash, Russell, and Brian Lake. *Bizarre Books.* London: Pavilion Books, 1998.

Ashmead, Larry. *Bertha Venation.* New York: HarperCollins, 2007.

Borgmann, Dmitri A. *Beyond Language: Adventures in Word and Thought.* New York: Charles Scribner's Sons, 1967.

——. *Language on Vacation: An Olio of Orthographical Oddities.* New York: Charles Scribner's Sons, 1965.

Brandreth, Gyles. *The Joy of Lex: An Amazing and Amusing Z to A and A to Z of Words.* London: Robson Books, 2002.

Burnam, Tom. *The Dictionary of Misinformation.* New York: Perennial Library, 1986.

Byrne, Josefa Heifetz, ed. *Mrs. Byrne's Dictionary of Unusual, Obscure and Preposterous Words.* Secaucus, NJ: Citadel, 1976.

Davies, Christopher. *Divided by a Common Language: A Guide to British and American English.* Sarasota, FL: Mayflower Press, 1997.

Dickson, Paul. *Dickson's Word Treasury.* New York: John Wiley & Sons, 1992.

——. *Labels for Locals: What to Call People from Abilene to Zimbabwe.* Springfield, MA: Merriam-Webster, 1997.

Diefendorf, David. *Amazing . . . But False!* New York: Sterling, 2007.

Dittrick, Mark. *Misnomers.* New York: Collier, 1986.

Donner, Michael. S. *Wordrow's Palindrome Encyclopedia: I Love

Me, Vol. I. Chapel Hill, NC: Algonquin Books of Chapel Hill, 1996.

Dunn, Jerry. *Idiom Savant: Slang As It Is Slung.* New York: Owl Books, 1997.

Eaton, Arthur Wentworth Hamilton. *Funny Epitaphs.* Boston: H. H. Carter & Karrick, 1885.

Eckler, Ross. *Making the Alphabet Dance.* New York: St. Martin's Griffin Edition, 1996.

——, ed. *The New Anagrammasia: A Collection of 8876 Anagrams and Antigrams Published between 1797 and 1991.* Morristown, NJ: Word Way's Monograph Series 2, 1991.

——, ed. *Word Recreations: Games and Diversions from Word Ways.* New York: Dover, 1980.

Edwards, Megan, and Mark Sedenquist. *Caution: Funny Signs Ahead.* Berkeley, CA: Ulysses Press, 2008.

Espy, Willard. *An Almanac of Words at Play.* New York: Crown Publishers, 1975.

——. *The Game of Words.* New York: Grosset & Dunlap, 1972.

Evans, Rod L. *The Artful Nuance: A Refined Guide to Imperfectly Understood Words in the English Language.* New York: Perigee, 2009.

——. *Sorry, Wrong Answer: Trivia Questions That Even Know-It-Alls Get Wrong.* New York: Perigee, 2010.

——. *Thingamajigs and Whatchamacallits: Unfamiliar Terms for Familiar Things.* New York: Perigee, 2011.

Evans, Rod L., and Irwin M. Berent. *Getting Your Words' Worth: Discovering and Enjoying Phantonyms, Gramograms, Anagrams, and Other Fascinating Word Phenomena.* New York: Warner Books, 1993.

Feldman, Gilda, and Phil Feldman. *Acronym Soup: A Stirring Guide to Our Newest Word Form.* New York: William Morrow, 1994.

Foss, Gwen. *The Confused Quote Book.* New York: Gramercy Books, 1997.

Frankel, Ken, and Robert Wilson. *Off the Wall: The Best Graffiti Off the Walls of America.* Marietta, GA: Longstreet Press, 1996.

Gallant, Frank K. *A Place Called Peculiar: Stories About Un-*

usual American Place-Names. Springfield, MA: Merriam-Webster, 1998.

Gardner, Martin, and Charles Bombaugh. *Oddities and Curiosities of Words and Literature*. Mineola, NY: Dover Publications, 1961.

Gove, Phillip B., ed. *Webster's Seventh New Collegiate Dictionary*. Springfield, MA: G. & C. Merriam, 1963.

Grambs, David. *Did I Say Something Wrong?* New York: Plume, 1993.

Green, Joey. *Contrary to Popular Belief*. New York: Broadway Books, 2005.

Grothe, Mardy, Dr. *Oxymoronica: Paradoxical Wit and Wisdom from History's Greatest Wordsmiths*. New York: HarperCollins, 2004.

Hauptman, Don. *Acronymania*. New York: Laurel, 1993.

———. *Cruel and Unusual Puns*. New York: Laurel, 1991.

Hughes, Patrick. *More on Oxymoron*. New York: Penguin, 1983.

Irvine, William. *If I Had a Hi-Fi*. New York: Laurel, 1992.

Joyce, James. *Finnegans Wake*. New York: Penguin, 1999.

Lederer, Richard. *Adventures of a Verbivore*. New York: Pocket Books, 1994.

———. *Anguished English*. New York: Dell, 1987.

———. *Crazy English: The Ultimate Joy Ride Through Our Language*. New York: Pocket Books, 1989.

———. *Fractured English*. New York: Pocket Books, 1996.

———. *Get Thee to a Punnery: An Anthology of Intentional Assaults Upon the English Language*. New York: Laurel, 1988.

———. *The Word Circus*. Springfield, MA: Merriam-Webster, 1998.

———. *The Play of Words: Fun & Games for Language Lovers*. New York: Pocket Books, 1990.

Lloyd, John, and John Mitchinson. *The Book of General Ignorance: Everything You Think You Know Is Wrong*. New York: Harmony, 2006.

Luff, Eric von der. *The Inscribed List of Why Librarians Are Crazy: Hilarious Real Names of Real People from Library Catalogs*. North Syracuse, NY: Gegensatz Press, 2008.

McWhirter, Norris. *The Guinness Book of Records*. New York: Sterling Publishing, 1989.

Michaelsen, O. V. *Never Odd or Even: Palindromes, Anagrams, & Other Tricks Words Can Do*. New York: Sterling Publishing, 2005.

———. *The Word Play Almanac*. New York: Sterling Publishing, 2002.

Mish, Frederick C., ed. *Merriam-Webster's Collegiate Dictionary*. Tenth edition. Springfield, MA: Merriam-Webster, 1994.

Morice, Dave. *Alphabet Avenue: Wordplay in the Fast Lane*. Chicago: Chicago Review Press, 1997.

———. *The Dictionary of Wordplay*. New York: Teachers and Writers Collaborative, 2001.

Newby, Peter. *The Mammoth Book of Word Games*. London: Pelham Books, 1990.

———. *Pears Advanced Word-Puzzler's Dictionary*. London: Pelham Books, 1987.

Petras, Ross, and Kathryn Petras. *The 776 Stupidest Things Even Said*. New York: Main Street Books, 1993.

Toseland, Martin. *The Ants Are My Friends: Misheard Lyrics, Malapropisms, Eggcorns, and Other Linguistic Gaffes*. London: Portico Books, 2007.

Train, John. *John Train's Most Remarkable Names*. New York: Clarkson N. Potter, 1985.

———. *Remarkable Words with Astonishing Origins*. New York: Clarkson N. Potter, 1980.

Walston, John. *The Buzzword Dictionary*. Oak Park, IL: Marion Street Press, 2006.

Webster's Third New International Dictionary of the English Language. Unabridged. Springfield, MA: Merriam-Webster, 1971.

Wines, J. A. *Mondegreens: A Book of Mishearings*. London: Michael O'Mara Books, 2007.

SELECTED WEBSITES

Acronym Finder
www.acronymfinder.com

The Anagram Engine
www.easypeasy.com/anagrams

Anagram Genius
www.anagramgenius.com

Anagrams.net
www.anagrams.net

A Barrel Full of Words
www.jimwegryn.com/Words/Words.php

A Collection of Word Oddities and Trivia
http://jeff560.tripod.com/words.html

The Eggcorn Database
http://eggcorns.lascribe.net

The Heteronym Homepage!
www-personal.umich.edu/~cellis/heteronym.html

I, Rearrangement Servant/Internet Anagram Server
http://wordsmith.org/anagram

Merriam-Webster Unabridged
http://merriam-websterunabridged.com

OneLook Dictionary Search
www.onelook.com

Pun of the Day
www.punoftheday.com

Richard Lederer's Verbivore
www.verbivore.com

Taxonomy of Wordplay
www.questrel.com/records.html

Urban Dictionary
www.urbandictionary.com

Word Spy
www.wordspy.com

Wordplay
http://people.sc.fsu.edu/~jburkardt/fun/wordplay/wordplay
  .html

The Wordplay Web Site
www.fun-with-words.com

YourDictionary
www.yourdictionary.com

Zaba Search
www.zabasearch.com

Zo's Palindromes
http://members.shaw.ca/ancienteyes/zospalindromesa.htm

Rod L. Evans, Ph.D., is a professor of philosophy at Old Dominion University in Norfolk, Virginia. He is the author of *Every Good Boy Deserves Fudge*; *The Artful Nuance*; *Sorry, Wrong Answer*; and *Thingamajigs and Whatcha-macallits*.